W9-ABZ-124

QC
A7
R43

DATE DUE

MAY 06 2013

other fawcett premier books by
isaac asimov:

realm of algebra
realm of numbers
an easy introduction to the slide rule
the search for the elements

isaac
asimov
realm of
measure

diagrams by robert belmore

KVCC KALAMAZOO VALLEY COMMUNITY COLLEGE LIBRARY

a fawcett premier book
fawcett publications, inc., greenwich, conn.
member of american book publishers council, inc.

34835

THIS BOOK CONTAINS THE COMPLETE TEXT OF THE ORIGINAL HARDCOVER EDITION.

A Fawcett Premier book reprinted by arrangement with Houghton Mifflin Company, Boston.

Copyright © 1960 by Isaac Asimov. All rights reserved including the right to reproduce this book or parts thereof in any form.

Library of Congress catalog card number: 60-9091

PRINTED IN THE UNITED STATES OF AMERICA

to my faithful readers,
in all gratitude

contents

Feet and Yards

THE FARMING REVOLUTION

About 10,000 years ago, a few groups of human beings slowly developed agriculture. This led to a tremendous change in man's way of life.

Before the development of agriculture, man hunted for his food or, at most, kept herds of cattle, sheep, or goats and wandered with them in search of fresh pasture. In either case, these animal keepers lived in small groups and without settled homes. They were nomads (an expression coming from a Greek word meaning "pasture").

Once people turned to farming, however, they had to stay with the crops, for of course the crops did not move. But if this limited their freedom, it also gave them certain advantages. On a particular stretch of land, more food could be grown in the form of grain than could possibly be kept in the form of animal herds. For that reason, more human beings could be supported on that stretch of land. Population grew much denser in agricultural communities than in areas across which nomads wandered.

This growth of population within fixed areas caused human beings to huddle together into villages. By keeping together, the quiet farmers were better protected from roving tribes which had not yet given up their nomadic way of life.

Nomads were always a menace, for their hunting kept them expert in horsemanship and the use of weapons, so they were better fighters than the farmers were, man for man. However, as farmers organized they built walls about their towns. They also developed armies with elaborate weapons that the simple nomads could not duplicate. In the long run, despite occasional setbacks, the farmers won out.

(The Biblical story of Cain and Abel reminds us of the ancient feud between farmer and nomad, and also of who the final victor was. In chapter 4, verse 2 of the Book of Genesis, the Bible says: "And Abel was a keeper of sheep, but Cain was a tiller of the ground." Since the early Hebrews were themselves nomads, they naturally made nomad Abel the hero, and farmer Cain the villain.)

Walled towns developed into cities. The secure supply of food that farming made possible gave some men leisure time to think so that arts and engineering developed and, eventually, writing. What we call "civilization" was born.

With civilization, there came a new necessity, that of measuring. In nomadic cultures, it was perhaps enough to be able to count—to count the sheep in a flock or the cattle in a herd.

With settled life, more was necessary. To build a house, for instance (instead of a nomad's tent), some sort of measurement was needed in order that timbers of the right length be used and that they be put together in the right way. It could be done by trial and error, of course, but a house built by measurement was finished more quickly, stood more strongly, and looked better, too.

City walls, temples, palaces, aqueducts, all needed accurate measurements even more than houses did. The Egyptian pyramids and the Greek temples show signs that the most delicate measurements were involved in their building.

Even the farms themselves required measurement. A particular farm might be marked off from its neighbor by stones as boundary markers, but suppose the stones were moved just a bit. Perhaps one farmer decided to move them bit by bit, on the quiet, to increase his own farm somewhat at the expense of his neighbor's. Or suppose the stones were not moved, but one of the farmers claimed they had been. Or suppose there were a flood (as there was every year in Egypt) which more or less wiped out landmarks.

Obviously, there would be perpetual quarreling and

feuding unless there were some way to fix farm boundaries and areas beyond dispute.

Then, too, as men lived close together in cities, they were bound to quarrel. Inevitably, a government had to be formed. Some man (or men) had to be entrusted with the making of laws to guide behavior and to act as judge to settle quarrels or punish lawbreaking. But governments had to be supported and that meant but one thing—taxes.

And taxes meant measurement again. In the days before money, an individual might be taxed so much grain or so much linen and that "so much" had to be measured. To be sure, counting might be sufficient for some tax purposes, as when a farmer was taxed one pig in ten. Even so, there are small pigs and large pigs. The farmer would want to give a small pig, the tax collector would want to take a large one. Again, something more than counting was needed.

When metals were discovered and bits of them were used in trade, measurement became more important than ever. A measurement in a length of cloth might not matter much one way or the other. A mismeasured beam of wood might not be too great a tragedy. But even a small mistake in measuring out a quantity of gold could mean a great loss.

For all these reasons, men and the governments of men were always interested in systems of measurement. And once such a system was developed, they would work constantly to improve it. Even in modern times, we are still refining our measurements. And although the world's nations quarrel so desperately that it would seem they could never agree on anything, all have been honestly co-operating in the establishment of international systems of measurement.

THE BODY'S MEASURING RODS

To measure something is not as easy as one might think. We have inherited a whole system of measurement which we learn in early life and come to use almost as second nature. But what if you had not learned the system? What would you do if you were asked how long an object was?

Chances are you would hold your hands apart, palms facing, and say, "About so long." Or, if the object were a small one, you might hold thumb and forefinger close together and say, "About so long." If the object were quite long, you might say, "From here to about the corner."

All this is very vague. Once writing was developed, it became necessary to record measurements—in title deeds to farms, for instance, or in tax lists. How do you write down a measurement made by holding the hands apart, or one made by saying that something was as long as from here to there?

It would be better to try to compare a length with something definite that everyone else would understand. The easiest thing would be to compare it with part of the body. Human beings are roughly the same size and everyone would understand how long a thing was if you said, "It's about as long as a man's arm."

A crucial point was reached when it occurred to someone that a distance much longer than a man's arm could be measured by noting how many times the man's arm

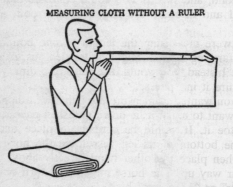

MEASURING CLOTH WITHOUT A RULER

could be stretched along that distance. For instance, a length of linen cloth could be held up against a man's arm, with one end at the shoulder. A mark could be made at the point where the tip of the man's fingers reached. That mark could be held up at the shoulder and a new mark made where the fingers now reached. This could be done over and over again and the conclusion might be that the total length of the cloth was equal to 17 times the length of the man's arm. Or, if you wanted to be short about it, you could say the stretch of linen was "17 armlengths" long.

Once this was done, all the techniques of arithmetic were available for measurement. A stretch of cloth 17 armlengths long was longer than another that was only 15 armlengths long. The two together would make 32 armlengths of cloth; you could divide either piece into even parts; and so on.

Of course, different types of measurement called for different systems. You wouldn't want to measure the length of a room by lying down and marking off the length of your arm from wall to wall. Even if you didn't mind the dirt and indignity of it, you would find it difficult to get your shoulder down at the exact point where your finger had made a mark.

It would be a lot simpler, in this case, to place the heel of one foot against the wall, put the heel of the other against the toe of the first, then move the first foot in front of the second, and so on. You could continue that to the other wall and measure the length of the room as, say, "17 feet."

If you were measuring the length of one boundary of a plot of farming land, it might be too tedious to mark it off in feet. Instead, you would take steps of ordinary length and measure it in "paces."

Or, if you wanted to measure the height of a horse, you wouldn't want to make it lie down and then pace it off, or heel-and-toe it. It would be simpler to place one hand against the bottom of its leg (assuming the horse to be gentle), then place the other hand directly above it, and work your way up. The horse might then turn out to be "17 hands" or "17 palms" high.

A number of words still exist in our language that represent measurements named after parts of the body. The most common one is the *foot,* which is approximately the length of a tall man's foot. The *hand* is by no means as common, but it is still used in England and America as the way of expressing the height of horses.

There are similar measurements which are now quite out of date, but which we occasionally come across in historical novels. There is the *digit*, which is a length equal to the width of a finger, and the *span*, which is the distance from the tip of the thumb to the tip of the little finger when the fingers are fully outstretched.

Then there is the *cubit*, an ancient measure which is familiar to us because it is used in the Bible. (The measurements of Noah's ark are given in cubits, for instance.) The word "cubit" comes from the Latin *cubitum* meaning

THE BODY'S MEASURING RODS

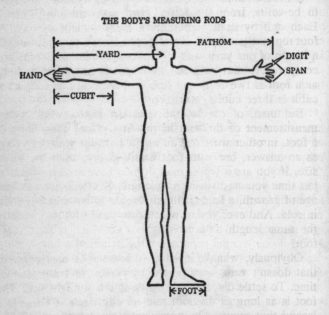

"elbow" and its length represents that from the elbow to the tip of the outstretched fingers. The old English measure, the *ell*, also comes from the word "elbow" but has come to be a much longer measurement than the cubit.

The *yard* may come from the same root as the word "girth" or "girdle" so perhaps it represents the distance about a man's waist (a slim man's waist, anyway). More likely, the word originally meant simply "measuring stick."

In the latter case, it might originally have represented half
the distance from fingertip to fingertip when the arms are
stretched out fully.

The full length, from fingertip to fingertip, of outstretched
arms is the *fathom*. This is from an Anglo-Saxon word
meaning "embrace," which is something you do, after all,
with the full length of your arms.

AGREEING ON THE VALUES

All these names for different types of measure are said
to be *units,* from the Latin word *unus* meaning "one."
Each unit by itself represents a measurement of one. A
foot represents a length equal to one foot; a yard represents
a length of one yard, and so on. Longer measurements are
compared to that unit. A length that is two times as long
as a foot is two feet; one that is three times as long as a
cubit is three cubits, and so on.

But then, of course, the question arises, what is the
measurement of the unit in the first place? How long is
a foot, in other words? You might hold up your own foot
as an answer, but your foot hasn't always been the same
size. If you are a young man, it may have grown since the
last time you used it as a measure. Even if you are past the
age of growth, a foot is slightly longer in hot weather than
in cold. And even if that weren't so, your foot isn't exactly
the same length as your neighbor's. Which is the "real"
foot?

Obviously, what is needed is some foot measurement
that doesn't vary from person to person or from time to
time. To settle disputes, the ruler of a city might say: The
foot is as long as my foot and no one else's. (There is a
legend that our foot was originally the length of the feet
of Charlemagne, who was a tall person. If the legend is
true, his feet were an inch and a quarter longer than mine.)

Or it might be proclaimed that the yard was the length
from the nose to the outstretched fingertip of the king.
(Again, there is a legend that King Henry I of England,
in the early 1100's, established the modern yard on his
own body in that way.)

By this means, a *standard measure* is agreed upon. It doesn't matter what the standard measure is as long as everyone concerned agrees.

A difficulty would arise, though, in the fact that it would be difficult to get the King of England to travel from village to village measuring out lengths of cloth from his nose to his fingertips. He would probably feel he was too busy for that. What is needed then is for the king to consent to have a stick held up against him so that a mark could be made at his nose and another at the fingertips. That would be a *standard yardstick*. The distance between the two marks would become the official yard.

Nobody would then be expected to make use of his own body or of anybody's body. The government, or some private manufacturer under government inspection, could produce quantities of sticks with measurements marked off by comparison with the standard yardstick and distribute one to each village. The village could use these *secondary standards* to check up on the yardsticks being used by the local merchants.

Obviously, there would always be a temptation for a merchant to shave off a bit of his yardstick. It might not be enough to notice, but in measuring yard after yard after yard, the discrepancy might mount up to a tidy profit. If no one noticed, he might shave off another bit and before long, all measurements would be in chaos.

Societies have always been interested in the control of measures and the preservation of fixed standards. During the Middle Ages, the guilds of tradesmen regulated themselves, since anyone who cheated hurt all the rest. Later on, governments took over, and set up standards of all sorts of measurements that were taken care of more and more elaborately. Stringent penalties were often imposed for false measure and officers were appointed to enforce them.

Here in the United States, at the present time, there is the National Bureau of Standards, which was established in 1901 to take care of our own standard measures. It has taken on many other duties since that time. It conducts research for the establishment of new measures, of improving the old, of guarding against false measure, and so on.

Our modern society must be even more concerned with accurate measure than any previous ones. The measurement of modern tools, machinery, and technical devices must be many times more accurate than anything our ancestors dreamed of. We have screws, bolts, wrenches, light-bulb sockets, wall plugs, and a thousand other things all made in certain identical measurements. It is only accurate measure that makes mass production possible. Without standard measures that all factories might use in common, our industrial and technological civilization would fall apart.

DOVETAILING THE UNITS

Once the notion of standard measures was worked out, people could (and did) use inanimate objects of all sorts as measuring rods. It became common to use sticks of a standard length, and we still do this, in our foot rules and yardsticks. Thus, it was quite natural that certain units of length with names like *rod* and *pole* came into use.

People engaged in special types of measurement might name units after the devices they used in measuring. For instance, surveyors used long chains to help them with their measurements of length. (A long chain could be folded into a small space, whereas a long stick would be hard to keep and to handle.) So surveyors had a unit they called the *chain,* and, also, of course, the *link.*

For small lengths, you could use a small inanimate object, like a grain of barley. This is called a *barleycorn* (the word "corn" being an old-fashioned version of our word "kernel"). The barleycorn is still used as the unit of shoe size. A size seven shoe is one barleycorn longer than a size six shoe.

This large number of different units to be used for one type of measurement (length) is useful in a way, since anyone can find a particular unit that suits him best. It is also useful in another way, too, that requires a little explanation.

Measuring units of lengths is not like counting people or animals. If you counted 31 head of cattle, you would know there were 31 and not 32 or 30. What's more, you would know there were exactly 31 and not 31.1 or 30.9.

Counting the units in a certain distance, however, would almost certainly not end up evenly. A length of cloth might be somewhat more than 31 yards long and yet not quite 32 yards long either. Today, our impulse would be to introduce fractions and say that the length was 31 1/2 yards long or 31 3/16 yards long.

But fractions are a rather sophisticated branch of mathematics. It is only because they are pounded into us in grammar school that we can use them as conveniently as we do (and some of us have our troubles at that). In early times, it was easier to avoid fractions by switching from a long unit to a shorter one.

For instance, a length of cloth might be 31 yards plus 1 foot plus 4 inches. The merchant could possibly decide this by laying his yardstick along the length 31 times, then reach for his foot rule to lay that off once, and finish by means of his small inch-gadget.

However, it would certainly be inconvenient to keep a number of standard measures about, switching from one to the other at need. How much more convenient it would be to mark off the yardstick into smaller sections representing feet and inches. We're used to this and take it for granted, but the first man (or men) who thought of doing so must have been ingenious indeed.

In order to do this, it would be most convenient if the smaller unit went into the larger one evenly. There's no reason it should, however. Why should the length of Charlemagne's foot go evenly into the distance from King Henry's nose to his fingertips? Nevertheless, for convenience' sake, the shorter unit might be adjusted slightly to make it fit the longer. In that way, one standard unit would serve for both.

For example, suppose you settle on the yard as the standard measure and agree to make all other measurements of length fit into it evenly one way or another. The foot is roughly a third of a yard in length, so agree that it be considered exactly a third of a yard. The yardstick can then be marked off into three equal parts and one of those parts becomes the standard foot. It may not be exactly

THREE FEET MAKE ONE YARDSTICK

equal to the original foot of Charlemagne, but that doesn't matter. As long as everyone agrees that three feet make a yard, that is all that counts.

Similarly, you can decide that exactly twelve inches make a foot and that a foot marked off into twelve equal parts will be made up of standard inches. (In fact, the word "inch" comes from a Latin word meaning "a twelfth.")

You can work upwards from the yard also, and allow for longer measures. You can make the fathom equal to two yards exactly.

Another example is the unit called the *furlong*. (This word is an abbreviation of "furrow-long," the length of a ploughed furrow, a direct indication of the connection between measures and farming.) The traditional length of a furlong must have been close to 220 yards, and it was eventually defined as exactly that.

In the same way, an inch was set equal to three barley-corns; a hand or palm to four inches, and a span to nine inches.

In one case at least, quite an adjustment had to be made to make a measurement fit into the scheme. The Romans, you see, counted off distances according to the paces of their marching legions. A thousand paces, they called *milia passuum,* which is Latin for "a thousand paces." This was shortened to *milia* and, in English, became *mile.*

A Roman pace was a trifle over five of our feet, so that the Roman mile was a trifle over 5000 feet. But once the English stabilized their units of length, a 5000-foot mile was inconvenient because it came out to an uneven number of furlongs—a little over 7 1/2 furlongs actually. So they decided to lengthen the mile in order to make it exactly 8 furlongs long, and now the "thousand-pace" distance is equal to about 1050 paces. It was for this reason, too, that the mile ended up being 1760 yards long or 5280 feet long, numbers that are not easy to remember.

Sometimes, a measurement will fit evenly with one unit but not with another. For instance, a yard is equal to just two cubits, but that means the cubit is equal to 1 1/2 feet. Again, a furlong is equal to just 40 rods, but that means a rod must be equal to 5 1/2 yards.

There are even worse examples. The surveyors set their unit, the chain, even with the mile. They let the mile be equal to just 80 chains, and each chain was set equal to 100 links. So far, so good, but once this was adjusted it turned out that the link didn't fit in evenly with the inch, foot, or yard. One link turned out to be equal to 7.92 inches.

However, even when the dovetailing wasn't perfect, the establishment of so many of one unit into another made it possible to apply arithmetic to measurements more intimately and successfully than ever. But it was a kind of arithmetic that wasn't quite the same as that used in counting.

Inches and Miles

CHANGING THE UNITS

Any two measures can be added or subtracted according to the ordinary rule of arithmetic, as long as the units used are the same for both measures. Thus, 7 inches plus 5 inches are 12 inches, just as surely as 7 apples and 5 apples are 12 apples.

However, can we add 2 feet and 6 inches? The sum of 2 and 6 is 8, but the sum of 2 feet and 6 inches is neither 8 feet nor 8 inches. This is something like trying to add 2 apples and 6 bananas. Certainly you cannot say that the answer is either 8 apples or 8 bananas.

The situation in the case of feet and inches is not quite the same as that of apples and bananas. Apples cannot be changed to bananas nor can bananas be changed to apples. For additions that include both, you are stuck. Feet, however can be changed to inches and inches can be changed to feet. If either change is made, 2 feet and 6 inches can be added together.

That is where the arithmetic of measurements differs from the ordinary arithmetic that deals with numbers only. In the arithmetic of measurement, the units must be handled as carefully as the numbers.

Thus, since 1 foot is equal to 12 inches, 2 feet must be equal to 2×12, or 24 inches. The sum of 2 feet and 6

THE ADVANTAGES OF MEASURING RODS

12 INCHES MAKE ONE FOOT RULE

inches is therefore equal to the sum of 24 inches and 6 inches. That is like adding apples to apples, and the answer is 30 inches.

You might work it the other way around, too. Since there are 12 inches in a foot, 6 inches (which is half of 12 inches) must be equal to 1/2 foot. The sum of 2 feet and 6 inches is therefore equal to the sum of 2 feet and 1/2 foot, which comes out to 2 1/2 feet.

Now you have two answers to the same problem, one being 2 1/2 feet and the other 30 inches, but this is no paradox. Since there are 12 inches to a foot, 2 1/2 feet must equal 2 1/2 × 12, or 30 inches. The two answers are the same length, after all, but merely express that length in different units. (The number which expresses a certain measurement varies with the unit you choose, but the number *combined* with the unit always remains the same measurement.)

In order to work out such problems, it is important to know just what the relationship is between two units. If you do not remember that there are 12 inches in a foot, you cannot add 2 feet and 6 inches. Of course, you do remember that fact, because it is drilled into you in grammar school and you make much use of it afterward. In the

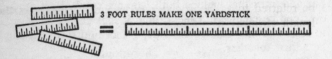

same way, you remember that there are 3 feet to a yard.

You might also remember that there are 36 inches in a yard, but you don't have to if you know the inch-foot and the foot-yard relationships. If you know that 1 foot equals 12 inches, you can substitute 12 inches for 1 foot wherever the latter occurs. Thus, when you say that 1 yard equals 3 feet, it is like saying that 1 yard is equal to 3 × 1 foot. Now substitute the 12 inches for the 1 foot (they're the same thing, after all) and you have the fact that 1 yard is equal to 3 × 12 inches, or to 36 inches.

In fact, if you happen to remember that there are 1760

yards in a mile, then you can easily calculate the number of inches in a mile. Since 1 yard equals 36 inches, when we say that 1 mile equals 1760 × 1 yard, we are saying that it equals 1760 × 36 inches, or 63,360 inches.

It works the other way around, too, if we reverse the procedure. To go from a larger unit to a smaller one, as we have just seen, we must multiply, since a given length contains more of the smaller unit than of the larger. To do the reverse—to go from a smaller unit to a larger—we must do the reverse of multiply; we must divide.

I have mentioned that there are 8 furlongs in a mile. If we know that there are 5280 feet in 1 mile, we can substitute 8 furlongs for one mile and say that there are 5280 feet in 8 furlongs. If we divide 5280 feet by 8 the answer will be 8 furlongs divided by 8. The quotient of 5280 feet divided by 8 is 660 feet while the quotient of 8 furlongs divided by 8 is 1 furlong. The solution then is that there are 660 feet in 1 furlong.

Gradually, as you make use of these measures, all these relationships become fixed in your mind. However, it doesn't hurt to have tables prepared to help beginners (and to help non-beginners, too, who sometimes need a bit of refreshing.)

For instance a table of *units of length* (which can also be referred to as *linear measure* because it measures the length of lines) would look like this:

1 mile	=	8 furlongs
1 furlong	=	40 rods
1 rod	=	5 1/2 yards
1 yard	=	3 feet
1 foot	=	12 inches

This really gives you all the information you need. To change miles into furlongs, you need only multiply the number of miles by 8. Thus, 19 miles is really 19 × 1 mile, from the table, you can change that to 19 × 8 furlongs, or 152 furlongs. To change miles into rods, you have to change the miles first into furlongs and then, by a further multiplication of 40, change the furlongs into rods.

Just to show this step by step, 19 miles equals 19×1 mile, which equals 19×8 furlongs, as I've said. But 19×8 furlongs is equivalent to saying $19 \times 8 \times 1$ furlong, and from the table we see we can replace that by $19 \times 8 \times 40$ rods. That comes out 6080 rods.

Without going through the steps, you probably see by now that to change miles to inches, you must multiply the number of miles first by 8 to get furlongs, then by 40 to get rods, then 5 1/2 to get yards, then by 3 to get feet, and finally by 12 to get inches. In this way 19 miles equals $19 \times 8 \times 40 \times 5 1/2 \times 3 \times 12$ or 1,203,840 inches.

To go from a smaller to a larger unit, you must divide, as I have already explained, and the table will guide you there, too. To go from inches to feet you must divide by 12. Thus 72 inches is equal to $72 \div 12$, or 6 feet. You can change inches to yards by dividing first by 12, then by 3, so that 72 inches would equal 2 yards, and so on.

EASING THE UNIT-CHANGE

Although the table of linear measures is adequate, there are ways of making it simpler.

For instance, is it absolutely necessary to arrange matters so that there must be repeated multiplications? These are tedious and increase the chances of making a mistake somewhere along the line.

Why not, instead, supply a table in which numbers are given that will convert a particular unit into any other unit? For instance, in the case of the mile, we can set up the following table:

1 mile =	8	furlongs
1 mile =	320	rods
1 mile =	1760	yards
1 mile =	5280	feet
1 mile =	63,360	inches

Now to convert a mile into any of the other ordinary units of length, we need simply multiply by the figure given. The number of miles multiplied by 8 will give the equivalent distance in furlongs. If the number of miles were multiplied by 320, we would have the distance in rods; by 1760, in yards, and so on.

These numbers are *conversion factors,* for by use of them one unit is converted into another.

A table such as the one just given uses conversion factors which are obtained by multiplying the factors given in the earlier table of linear measure on page 23. For instance, there are 8 furlongs in a mile, 40 rods in a furlong, and 5 1/2 yards in a rod; therefore, the number of yards in a mile is 5 1/2 × 40 × 8, or 1760. Since there are 3 feet in a yard, the number of feet in a mile is 3 × 1760, or 5280.

Thus, the conversion factors for the mile, as given in the table, do some of our multiplying for us. To convert 19 miles into inches, we need not multiply 19 by 8 × 40 × 5 1/2 × 3 × 12, but merely by 63,360, which is the pre-calculated product of 8 × 40 × 5 1/2 × 3 × 12.

I have chosen the mile as the demonstration unit because it is the longest of the ordinary units of length. To change it to any other unit requires multiplication by some figure or other.

In changing a smaller unit to a larger one, though, division is necessary. To change rods to furlongs means dividing by 40; that is, 1 rod = furlong ÷ 40. Of course, dividing by 40 is the same as multiplying by 1/40, so we can write the conversion: 1 rod = 1/40 furlong. However, that is no help. If we try to multiply by 1/40, as it stands, our only method is to divide by 40. Thus 76 rods equals 76/40 or 1.9 furlongs.

But suppose we convert 1/40 into a decimal fraction; 1/40, after all, is equal to 0.025. Instead of dividing by 40, it is now possible to multiply by 0.025. You would get the same answer: 76 × 0.025 = 1.9.

You might ask: What is the advantage?

To be sure, it might seem easier to divide by 40 than to multiply by 0.025. However, suppose you wanted, for some reason, to convert a length given in inches into the same length given in miles. The way to do it, from the information given so far in this book, is to divide the number of inches by 63,360. Well, consider the length of

41,267 inches. Dividing that number by 63,360 is not an impossible task, but it is tedious and troublesome.

Now consider the fact that the fraction 1/63,360 can be converted into the decimal 0.00001578. Suppose you multiply 41,267 by 0.00001578. The multiplication is also tedious, but if you try both procedures, I think you will agree that the multiplication is not nearly as bad as the division. (If you're curious, 41,267 inches is equal to 0.6513 miles, worked out either way.)

In general, people engaged in routine computations would almost always prefer to multiply rather than to divide. For that reason, in preparing conversion factors for turning small units into larger ones, the decimals are always used. (Of course, to prepare the decimal, one must first work it out and that involves a division. But it is like doing the division once and for all to begin with, as $1.00 \div 40 = 0.025$, and never having to do it again.)

An example of a table including decimal conversion factors is:

1 inch	= 0.08333	foot
1 inch	= 0.02778	yard
1 inch	= 0.005051	rod
1 inch	= 0.0001263	furlong
1 inch	= 0.00001578	mile

One difficulty about conversion factors so expressed is that the decimals do not necessarily come out even. In the case of $1/40 = 0.025$, it does. The value is exactly equal to 1/40. But, on the other hand, 1 inch = 1/12 of a foot exactly, and what is 1/12 in decimal form? It is 0.083333-33333. . . . and so on indefinitely. There is no way of expressing 1/12 exactly in decimal form.

However, the more places you use, the closer you come to exactness. For instance 264 inches equal 264/12, or exactly 22 feet. On the other hand, 264×0.083 is equal to 21.912. But $264 \times 0.0833 = 21.9912$, and $264 \times 0.08333 = 21.99912$. The difference between the product of 264×0.8333 and the quotient of $264 \div 12$ isn't enough to worry about. And if you were doing such fine work that it were, you need simply carry out the decimal conversion figure a few more places and cut the differences still further.

In the same way, if 0.00001578 isn't accurate enough as a conversion factor for inches to miles to suit your needs, you can calculate the fraction 1/63,360 to one more place and make it 0.000015783. Or you could calculate it to two more places and make it 0.0000157828, and so on.

Naturally, in the few cases where it is easier to divide than to multiply, there is no reason why you should not. In converting feet to yards, it is far easier to divide by 3 than to multiply by 0.3333. It is even easier to divide by 12 in converting inches to feet than to multiply by 0.08333. In those cases, divide by all means. However, you will find by experience that such easy divisions are very much the exception in dealing with unit conversions, and in this book I will always give conversion factors as decimals to multiply rather than as whole numbers to divide, even when the division is easier.

CONVERSIONS BY TABLE

It is easy enough to prepare a set of conversion factors for every unit of length, as I have done for the mile and for the inch. Then, anyone working with unit-changes need only shuffle the table till he finds the one he wants. Human nature being what it is, however, he will resent the necessity of shuffling. Is there no way of preparing all the information in a single table?

There is, and one is prepared for you here, by which you can find the conversion factors that will convert miles, furlongs, rods, yards, feet, or inches into miles, furlongs, rods, yards, feet, or inches in any combination.

Using such a table you can convert miles to rods as follows: Locate "mile" on the left and run your finger horizontally along that row until you come to the column headed "rod." The number at this point is 320. That is the conversion factor for miles to rods. The number of miles multiplied by 320 gives the number of rods. To convert rods to miles, start "rod" on the left and run your finger along that row until you come to the column headed "mile." The figure there is 0.003125. The number of rods multiplied by 0.003125 will give you the number of miles.

Any figure in the table will convert the unit of its horizontal row into the unit of its vertical column. Notice, too, that wherever both row and column belong to the same unit, as where the "yard" column crosses the "yard" row, the conversion factor is given as 1. This makes sense. If you multiply the number of yards by 1, you still have the number of yards. The factor 1 "converts" miles into miles, yards into yards, and so on.

Any set of similar units can be prepared in the form of such a table, but often these tables are not really needed in full. For instance one practically never wishes to convert miles into inches, or inches into miles, so that though conversion factors can be prepared for the purpose and can be used, they hardly ever are. They remain curiosities.

Rather, one would want to know, particularly, conversion factors for units that are close together, where similar distances might be expressed at times in one unit, at times in another. For instance, you might speak of a carpet as being 12 feet long at one time, and as being 4 yards long at another. Both measurements are the same and the conversion factor is so simple that this inconsistency hardly worries anyone.

However, a piece of property might be so many yards long or so many rods long. Here a conversion factor is involved that is not so easy to handle, and there could be confusion. Therefore, there is reason to make a special effort to learn those factors, if you are likely to be dealing in yards and rods. Thus:

$$1 \text{ rod } = 5.5 \quad \text{yards}$$
$$1 \text{ yard } = 0.1818 \text{ rod}$$

Thus, a piece of land that is 14.5 rods long would be 14.5 × 5.5, or 79.75 yards long. On the other hand a piece of land which was 100 yards long would be 100 × 0.1818, or 18.18 rods long.

	mile	furlong	rod	yard	foot	inch
mile	1	8	320	1760	5280	63,360
furlong	0.125	1	40	220	660	7920
rod	0.003125	0.0125	1	5.5	16.5	198
yard	0.0005682	0.004545	0.1818	1	3	36
foot	0.0001894	0.001515	0.0606	0.3333	1	12
inch	0.00001578	0.0001263	0.005051	0.02778	0.08333	1

INTRODUCING THE STRANGE UNIT

The table need not be restricted only to the ordinary units of linear measure. Any unit, however unusual or strange, can be introduced into the table, provided it is a unit of length.

Take the surveyor's units of length, for instance, which I have already mentioned. A chain is equal to 1/80 of a mile. Since a mile is equal to 5280 feet, the chain is equal to 5280/80 or 66 feet. It is therefore equal to 66/3 or 22 yards, and to 22/5.5 or 4 rods. Working from unit to unit, all the conversion factors can be calculated, and the chain can be included in the table of linear measure. A chain is equal to 100 links, so a link is equal to 0.66 foot, 0.22 yard, 0.04 rod, and so on. The link, too, can be introduced into the table.

Nevertheless, although this can be done, the surveyor may find it unnecessary to go that far. When it comes to conversions, a surveyor may find that most of the time he will be bouncing back and forth between chains and yards; and between links, feet, and inches. The following table may suit him and be sufficient for almost all his work:

$$
\begin{array}{rcl}
1 \text{ chain} &=& 22 \text{ yards} \\
1 \text{ yard} &=& 0.04545 \text{ chain} \\
1 \text{ link} &=& 0.66 \text{ foot} \\
1 \text{ foot} &=& 1.5151 \text{ links} \\
1 \text{ link} &=& 7.92 \text{ inches} \\
1 \text{ inch} &=& 0.1265 \text{ link}
\end{array}
$$

As another example, the *international nautical mile,* a unit of length used at sea by ships of almost all nations, is somewhat longer than the ordinary mile (sometimes called the *statute mile*). Whereas the statute mile is 5280 feet long, the nautical mile is 6076.1 feet long. (There's a story to that odd number of feet which I will explain in the next chapter.) To anyone who must deal with distance on both land and sea, it would be interesting to know that:

$$
\begin{array}{rcl}
1 \text{ nautical mile} &=& 1.1508 \text{ statute miles} \\
1 \text{ statute mile} &=& 0.8693 \text{ nautical miles}
\end{array}
$$

Other conversion factors involving the nautical mile would be less important.

Another unit of length used at sea, by the way, is the *league*. This is a measure dating back to medieval times, when different parts of Europe had their own "leagues" of varying size. Some were as short as 2 1/2 miles, some as long as 4 1/2 miles. (The "seven-league boots" of fairy-tales, therefore, must have enabled those wearing them—usually ogres—to take steps anywhere from 17 to 31 miles long, depending on the locale of the tale.)

Nowadays, though, the league is set equal to 3 nautical miles. Therefore:

$$1 \text{ league} = 3.4524 \text{ statute miles}$$
$$1 \text{ statute mile} = 0.2898 \text{ league}$$

When Captain Nemo, in Jules Verne's book, traveled "twenty thousand leagues under the sea," he had traveled $20,000 \times 3.4524$, or just about 69,000 miles.

(Another uncommon measure used by seamen is the *fathom* or "double-yard" for measuring depth of water. When Shakespeare writes, "Full fathom five thy father lies," he implies drowning in thirty feet of water.)

The measures I have included in the table on page 29 are said to belong to the *English system,* because they originated in England. They are also referred to as the *common system* (in those countries that use them) because they are commonly used in everyday life. The common system is used in Great Britain, the United States, Canada, South Africa, Australia, and New Zealand. I'll refer to these countries in this book as the "English-speaking countries."

The other units I have introduced, involving surveyor's measure and nautical measure, are also used in the English-speaking countries. There is no reason, however, why foreign measures can't be worked into this system where necessary. For instance, a common measure of length in Russia is the *verst*. It is about 3500 feet long. Consequently:

$$1 \text{ mile} = 1.5085 \text{ versts}$$
$$1 \text{ verst} = 0.6629 \text{ mile}$$

If you are reading a Russian book which gives a distance as 140 versts, you know that this distance is 140 × 0.6629, or 92.8 miles. You can work out the conversion factors between versts and the other common units and even include it in the table if you wish.

I think these are enough examples to show you that conversion factors can tie any unit of length with any other units of length. Nevertheless, although conversion factors are a complete answer, they are not an entirely satisfactory one—at least as I have given them in this chapter. They are so uneven and unpredictable.

To be sure, you can simplify them for ordinary purposes. If you decide that 1 league is equal to 3 1/2 statute miles, or that 1 statute mile is equal to 7/8 nautical mile, or that 1 verst equals 2/3 mile, you will be close enough for most purposes.

Even so, conversion figures in the common system are a troublesome lot. Despite all the drill in school, few of us can convert one unit into another without hesitation. And some of the common units have been almost completely wiped out because people would rather forget them than try to use them. Have you ever used the rod or the furlong, for instance?

Well, surely, you might think, the ingenuity of man can work out a better system. If you think so, you are right. The ingenuity of man has indeed worked out a better system, and this was done a hundred and fifty years ago. Unfortunately, we, in the English-speaking countries, have chosen not to benefit from it.

Centimeters and Kilometers

MEASURING THE EARTH

The story of the "better system" begins in the 1700's, when scientists were trying to make accurate measurements of the earth's surface. After the great exploring voyages of the 1500's and 1600's, the geography of the whole earth was known in outline. However, to make long sea voyages as safe as possible it was necessary to devise maps that were more and more accurate.

Furthermore, there was a great deal of scientific interest in the exact shape of the earth. The great English scientist Isaac Newton had predicted, from his theories, that the earth was not an exact sphere, but was slightly flattened at the poles. That is, a line extending through the center of the earth from North Pole to South Pole would be a trifle shorter than a line extending through the center of the earth from a point on the equator to an opposite point on the equator. Other scientists contended that, on the contrary, the earth bulged at the poles.

There was great importance in knowing whether Newton or his adversaries were correct. Basic scientific theories depended upon it. Besides, accurate maps could not be drawn unless it were known whether the earth was bulged or flattened at the poles, and by how much.

The question could be decided if careful measurements were made of the curvature of the earth at spots near the poles and at other spots near the equator. If the earth showed less curvature near the poles, the poles were flattened; if the earth showed more curvature near the poles, the poles bulged.

In 1735, two French expeditions were sent out to Lapland and to Peru to make the necessary measurements of curvature. The difference in curvature was expected to be very slight and the measurements would therefore have to be very accurate. Naturally, both expeditions had to use precisely the same standard measure of length.

Each expedition took duplicate metal standards, adjusted to equality with each other as nearly as possible. These standards were supposed to be checked against each other afterward, also, to make sure there was no slight change during the two to three years the expeditions were away. However, one of the standards was accidentally dropped in sea water and rusted, so that the exact position of the marks, measuring the standard length, couldn't be checked.

Even so, the expeditions were successful. The earth's surface seemed definitely less curved in Lapland than in Peru (and later measurements have confirmed this). This meant that the earth was flattened at the poles and that Newton was right.

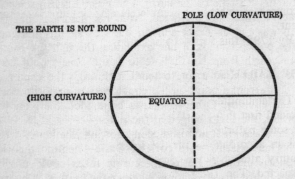

THE EARTH IS NOT ROUND

POLE (LOW CURVATURE)

(HIGH CURVATURE)

EQUATOR

What was even more important, though, was that the whole project clearly demonstrated the fact that science was advancing to the point where measurements could be made (and needed to be made) that were far better than the standards of measure then existing. New standards were needed very badly—standards that would be accepted by scientists of all nations. In fact, a whole new system of measures, especially designed to suit the needs of science, was needed.

This was quite clear to a number of people. For instance, the celebrated English architect Christopher Wren, who rebuilt much of London after the great fire of 1666, favored a reform of the system of measures. So did Thomas Jefferson, who was not only a great American statesman, but also an amateur scientist of considerable ability.

The trouble is, though, that people are very conservative about changing things they are used to, even when the change would be for their own good. (For instance, there are continual proposals for calendar reform these days— a reform is much needed. There are organizations pushing it, the United Nations is considering it, but nothing is being done, and I suspect that nothing will be done.)

Nothing was done about reforming standards of measure until there was a major upset and that was the French Revolution of 1789. At the time, France was the cultural leader of the West, so what she did was important. Moreover, the revolutionary leaders were anxious to break with the past. One of the things they did, then, was to appoint a committee to set up a completely new system of measurement.

By 1795, this was accomplished.

THE EARTH AS STANDARD

The committee which met to work out the new system decided first that the basic unit of length was to be based on some natural measurement, some fact of nature. This was in accordance with the spirit of the age, for in the century after Newton, science had grown popular and respected. The 1700's are often referred to as the "Age of Reason."

Since the glamorous scientific project of the time was the measurement of the earth, it was there that the committee turned. They began with the length of the distance from the equator to the North Pole (on a straight line running through Paris). Since this was a distance that was one-quarter the way around the earth, it is called the *quadrant* from a Latin word meaning "one quarter." To make sure of this distance, the committee set surveyors to work measuring distances in France and Spain out of which the length of the quadrant could be accurately determined.

A ten-millionth of the quadrant seemed to be a convenient length for everyday use and this was taken as the basic unit. This ten-millionth of a quadrant was named *mètre* (in French, of course) and we call it *meter* in English. The word is from the Latin *metrum* and Greek *metron,* both meaning simply "measure."

The system based on the meter is called the *metric system*.

But alas for human plans! The earth itself was intended to be the fundamental standard of length. However, once meter-sticks were manufactured and used, and after all sorts of measurements had been made on the basis of the length of the meter, it turned out that the length of the quadrant was just a trifle greater than the originators of the metric system had thought it was.

If the meter was exactly a ten-millionth of a quadrant, then the distance from the equator to the North pole would be equal to just 10,000,000 meters. But this is not so. The distance turns out to be 10,002,288.3 meters. It was far too late to change the meter's length. Too much had been done with it. Instead, the earth had to be abandoned as a standard.

In 1875, this was done. An international agreement set up the International Bureau of Weights and Measures. This group prepared a bar out of platinum-iridium alloy, an alloy which is extremely resistant to rust and change. Two fine marks were made on it and the distance between those two marks was considered to be the standard length of the meter.

The bar is called the *International Prototype Meter*. Each country adhering to the treaty was given a copy of this standard, the copies being called *National Prototype Meters*. The International Prototype Meter itself is kept at Sèvres, a suburb of Paris, under truly international control and is treated with the greatest possible care.

It is a pity that the meter turned out, after all, to be just an arbitrary length, and not based on a fact of nature as originally intended. However, attempts are being made to return to that principle.

Light behaves as though it consisted of tiny waves of energy, and, in the twentieth century, accurate measurements were made of the lengths of those waves. For instance, an element named cadmium gives off a red light when heated. The length of a single wave of this red light has been measured as equal to 0.00000064384696 meter.

In 1927, the Seventh General International Conference on Weights and Measures suggested that this wave length be accepted as the standard measure of length. If it were, then the International Prototype Meter would be equal to 1,553,164.13 wave lengths of cadmium red light. Then, even if that meter and all other standard meters were destroyed, science would still have its standard, a more fundamental and indestructible one than any man could make.

Later still, the green light given off by a particular type of mercury atom was suggested as the standard. Its wave length could be determined with an accuracy even greater than that of the cadimum red light. In either case, the important fact is this: mankind need no longer worry about standards of measurement.

Before leaving the subject, however, I would like to point out that one of the units in the common system is based on the size of the earth. It comes about this way.

All circles, from the smallest to the largest, have their circumferences divided into 360 *degrees* (from a Latin word meaning "down steps"). This division originated with the Babylonians, who noted that the sun took 365 days to make a complete circuit of the sky. If they divided the circle of the sky into 365 equal parts, the sun would move through one of those parts each day.

However, 365 is an inconvenient number, and the Babylonians chose to divide the circle into 360 parts instead. That was close enough and more convenient since 360 could be divided evenly by 2, 3, 4, 5, 6, 8, 9, 10, 12, 15, 18, 20, 24, 30, 36, 40, 45, 60, 72, 90, 120, and 180. To early civilizations that had not worked out convenient ways of handling fractions, such even divisions (which did not result in fractions) were very convenient. In contrast, 365 can be divided evenly only by 5 and 73.

Each degree was divided into 60 *minutes* and each minute into 60 *seconds*. (There are also a number of ways of dividing 60 evenly, so that number, too, was a great favorite with the Babylonians.) This system is called *angular measure,* because it can be used to measure angles as well as circumferences (and is used for both purposes to this day). It may be summarized as follows:

$$1 \text{ circle } = 360 \text{ degrees}$$
$$1 \text{ degree } = 60 \text{ minutes}$$
$$1 \text{ minute } = 60 \text{ seconds}$$

Now the circumference of the earth can be (and is) divided into degrees, minutes, and seconds, as any other circumference can be. The number of minutes composing the circumference of the earth (or any other circle) is 360×60, or 21,600. The nautical mile (which I mentioned in the previous chapter) is defined as equal to the length of one minute along the earth's circumference. This would make the nautical mile 1/21,600 or 0.0000464 of the earth's circumference.

The earth's circumference varies in length depending on whether it is measured about the equator, across the poles, or somewhere in between, because of the flattening at the poles. However the quadrant used by the founders of the metric system can be used, and along that line, one minute is equal to about 6076.097 feet. That length was set equal to the *International Nautical Mile* by the International Hydrographic Bureau, and many nations have accepted that value. (I promised in the previous chapter to tell you why a nautical mile was made up of such an uneven number of feet. This is why.)

The British, who always seem to go their own way, have decided to use the more even value of 6080 feet and that length makes up an *Admiralty mile.* This name comes from the fact that since the nautical mile is used at sea, it is of particular concern to the British Admiralty, which is in charge of the navy.

The most interesting thing about the nautical mile is that the length of the quadrant, which despite all attempts, does not come out even in meters (or in ordinary statute miles, either), does come out even in nautical miles. The quadrant is equal to 10,002,288.3 meters and to 6215.12 statute miles, but is equal to just 5400 nautical miles. Because of this dependence on a fact of geography, the nautical mile is sometimes called the *geographic mile*.

THE METRIC TABLE

The nautical mile, though based on a fact of nature, exists all by itself, so to speak. The meter, on the other hand, which misses being based on a fact of nature, serves as the basis for a whole series of interlocking measurements. The meter is therefore infinitely more important and useful than the nautical mile.

For instance, the meter has to be divided into smaller units and built up into larger ones, just as yards are divided into feet and inches and built up into furlongs and miles.

The French committee, however, didn't have other measures already existing that had to be squeezed into the system willy-nilly at the cost of odd conversion factors. The committee was starting from scratch and they made up the simplest possible table of conversion factors they could think of.

To do this, they used factors built up out of the number 10. Thus, the meter was divided into 10 *decimeters* (the prefix "deci-" coming from the Latin word for "ten"). The decimeter was divided into 10 *centimeters,* so that the meter was equal to 10×10, or 100 centimeters (the prefix "centi-" comes from the Latin word for "hundred"). The centimeter in turn was divided into 10 *millimeters* so that the meter was equal to $10 \times 10 \times 10$, or 1000 millimeters (and the prefix "milli-" is from the Latin word for "thousand").

Working it the other way, there are 10 meters in a *dekameter.* (Here, for units longer than a meter, the prefixes switch from Latin to Greek. "Deka-" is from the Greek word for "ten.") There are 10 dekameters in a *hectometer,* so that there are 10 × 10 or 100 meters in a hectometer (the prefix "hecto-" comes from the Greek word for "hundred"). Again, there are 10 hectometers in a kilometer so that there are 10 × 10 × 10 or 1000 meters in a kilometer (and the prefix "kilo-" comes from the Greek word for "thousand").

To summarize:

$$
\begin{array}{rcl}
1\ \text{kilometer} &=& 10\ \text{hectometers} \\
1\ \text{hectometer} &=& 10\ \text{dekameters} \\
1\ \text{dekameter} &=& 10\ \text{meters} \\
1\ \text{meter} &=& 10\ \text{decimeters} \\
1\ \text{decimeter} &=& 10\ \text{centimeters} \\
1\ \text{centimeter} &=& 10\ \text{millimeters}
\end{array}
$$

With this information, we can set up a table of metric units of length, with conversion factors to change any of the above units into any other. This table is as given here.

Compare this table of the metric units of length, with the table of the common units given on page 29. Do you see the difference? The conversion factors in the metric

METER STICK

YARDSTICK

system are all in powers of ten. All the conversion factors are exact and there are no inconvenient decimals.

In fact, since our system of numbers is based on ten, it is not even necessary to multiply or divide in making conversions among metric units of length. You need only move the decimal point.

Thus 0.001254 kilometer is equal to 0.01254 hectometer which is equal to 0.1254 dekameter, which is equal to 1.254 meters, which is equal to 12.54 decimeters, which is equal to 125.4 centimeters, which is equal to 1254 millimeters.

In working from large units to small, the decimal point

	kilometer	hectometer	dekameter	meter	decimeter	centimeter	millimeter
kilometer	1	10	100	1000	10,000	100,000	1,000,000
hectometer	0.1	1	10	100	1000	10,000	100,000
dekameter	0.01	0.1	1	10	100	1000	10,000
meter	0.001	0.01	0.1	1	10	100	1000
decimeter	0.0001	0.001	0.01	0.1	1	10	100
centimeter	0.00001	0.0001	0.001	0.01	0.1	1	10
millimeter	0.000001	0.00001	0.0001	0.001	0.01	0.1	1

was moved to the right. In working from small units to large, it must be moved to the left.

BELOW AND ABOVE

The units listed in the table just given are the common, everyday metric units of length. The demands of science, however, have forced an extension below the millimeter and above the kilometer.

For instance, people who work with cells, bacteria, viruses, and other microscopic objects find it useful to deal with the *micrometer,* which is one thousandth of a millimeter. (The prefix "micro-" comes from a Greek word meaning "small.") This unit is very commonly abbreviated to *micron,* but I think that is sloppy because it hides its relationship to the meter.

A thousandth of a micrometer is naturally called a *millimicrometer,* a unit which is invariably abbreviated to *millimicron.* The millimicrometer is a billionth of a meter and in 1960, the National Bureau of Standards adopted the prefix "nano-" for a billionth. The millimicrometer may therefore be called the *nanometer.* This unit is small enough to be used conveniently in measuring the lengths of light waves. The Swedish astronomer Anders Jonas Ångstrom suggested, in the 1860's, that a tenth of a millimicrometer be used for this purpose. That length could be called a "decimillimicrometer," I suppose, but no one ever uses that term. It is called simply an *Ångstrom unit,* in honor of the astronomer. Again, no one can tell from the name what the relationship is to the meter, but the thing is done, and cannot be changed.

A more logical subdivision of the millimicrometer is a thousandth of it (that is, a hundredth of an Ångstrom unit), which is naturally called a *micromicrometer.* "Micromicro" means "a millionth of a millionth" of a meter, which is just the size of the unit. In the English system of numbering, "a millionth of a millionth" is a "billionth." Although a "millionth of a millionth" is a "trillionth" in the American system, the British have begun to call a micromicrometer a *bicron,* the "bi-" referring to "billionth." The new prefix adopted for a trillionth by the National Bureau of Standards is "pico-" so a micromicrometer may be called a *picometer*.

For measuring the length of X-ray waves (which are much smaller than the waves of ordinary light), a unit only one thousandth of an Ångstrom unit (or one tenth of a micromicrometer) has been suggested and this is called an *X-unit*. Finally, it has been suggested that a unit equal in size to one hundredth of an X-unit be named the *fermi* (after Enrico Fermi, the Italian nuclear physicist who was one of those involved in the development of the atomic bomb). The fermi is a unit small enough to be used conveniently in measuring the sizes of such objects as protons and electrons, the smallest things known to science.

These small units can be summarized as follows:

1 millimeter	= 1000 micrometers (microns)
1 micrometer	= 1000 millimicrometers (millimicrons or nanometers)
1 millimicrometer	= 10 Ångstrom units
1 Ångstrom unit	= 100 micromicrometers (bicrons or picometers)
1 micromicrometer	= 10 X-units
1 X-unit	= 100 fermis

(In comparison, there are few units smaller than the inch in the common system. There is the barleycorn, which, as I said earlier in the book, is equal to 1/3 of an inch. There is also the *mil,* which is equal to one thousandth of an inch. This is used mostly by metalworkers who must deal with the measurements of fine wires.)

Now suppose we work the other way—upward from the kilometer. A length equal to 10 kilometers is sometimes called the *myriameter* ("myria-" coming from a Greek word meaning "ten thousand") while 100 myriameters (equal to 1000 kilometers) is a *megameter*. "Mega-" comes from a Greek word meaning "large." The National Bureau of Standards has adopted the prefix "giga-" for a billion units and "tera-" for a trillion units, so 1000 megameters is a *gigameter* and 1000 gigameters is a *terameter*. (These new prefixes had been adopted in 1958 by the International Committee on Weights and Measures, at Paris.)

(In contrast, the system of common units has no unit of length larger than the mile, except for the league.)

Actually, these higher metric units of length are never used. Most people are satisfied to use kilometers and find them convenient enough. Astronomers the world over, who must deal with stupendous distances, find even the megameter too short. Instead, they make use of the *light-year,* which is the distance light will travel in a year. Since light travels with extraordinary speed (in one second, it travels 186,272 miles) the light-year is a tremendous distance. It comes out to about 5,878,000,000,000 miles or 9464 terameters.

A still longer unit is the *parsec* which, for reasons there is no room to go into here, is equal to 3.26 light-years. This makes it equal to 19,161,000,000,000 miles or to 30,860 terameters.

The light-year and the parsec are not part of the metric system. However, they are based on facts of nature that are important to astronomers and they are useful measures.

RESISTING THE GOOD

The odd conversion factors present in the common system mean that school children in the English-speaking countries must spend countless hours learning the interrelationships of the units. What's more, despite all those hours, they never learn the interrelationships really well. School children in France and in other countries that have adopted the metric system have no trouble with their convenient conversion factors. They learn them quickly and permanently.

You might think that once the metric system was established, nations would fall over themselves in their hurry to change from old, foolish systems to one so strictly and simply logical. They did not, however, human nature being as conservative as it is. The metric system wasn't accepted without a struggle even in France.

Although the metric system was made compulsory in France in 1801, many Frenchmen insisted on using their old and illogical measures just because they were used to them. In 1837, France had to pass a law absolutely forbidding the use of any measures except the metric system after January, 1840, under the pain of stiff penalties.

Other nations slowly fell into line, one by one, and adopted the metric system. Even nations with non-European cultures, like India and Japan, now use it. Only the English-speaking nations do not.

Great Britain, at the time the metric system was first developed, was at war with France. It was in a life-and-death struggle against first the Revolutionaries and then against Napoleon. The British were in no mood to accept anything from the enemy. Besides, they have always been fond of their good old ways and have made almost a religion out of tradition. It seems, sometimes, that it doesn't matter how illogical a thing is; the British will go along with it if their grandfathers had anything to do with it. So they stuck to feet and yards and all the rest.

The United States went along with the measures it had inherited from England, but less enthusiastically. There were times when the Congress almost established the metric system in this country, but always the necessary law failed of passage, once by only a hair. And as time passed, it became harder and harder to make the switch.

You see, in order to change from common units to metric units, a great deal of overhaul must be done in tools and machinery. Devices which are adjusted to turn out objects just an inch wide would have to be readjusted to turn out objects that measure evenly in the metric system. It would mean a great investment to begin with, but this would be paid back eventually because of the greater simplicity and economy of the metric system.

However, the longer the United States waited, the more industrialized it became, the more intricate its plants and machinery grew. The initial investment and confusion that would result from the switchover became greater and greater. Now, in the second half of the twentieth century, many engineers and industrialists insist we cannot stop to make the change. We did not change when we could and now it is too late.

British and American scientists, to be sure, use the metric system in their scientific work. They have to. Not only is it ideally suited for scientific measurements, but our scientists dare not penalize themselves and science by using measurements the rest of the world would not understand. The result of that is, however, that British and American scientists must learn two systems of measurement—the common system as children, the metric system as adults.

Since the metric system is learned in later years, the British and American scientists are never quite as at home with it as are their colleagues in other countries. Again we lose out, and just in the area we can least afford to nowadays.

But is it really too late to make the change? Perhaps not, if we could decide on ways to introduce the metric system gradually.

To begin with, for instance, the metric system ought to be taught in grade school. If American children were made familiar with it they would, as adults, not find it so strange and foreign.

Then, little by little, metric measurements should be introduced into common use, without necessarily replacing the common measurements. For instance, distance between cities might be given in both kilometers and miles on road maps. Real estate transactions could give lot measurements in both meters and yards.

This would be clumsy, of course, since for a while we would be using two languages of measurement. In Canada, it is often necessary to print signs and documents in both French and English. In Switzerland, signs and documents must be printed in French, German, Italian, and Romansch. They've managed for centuries; we could manage for a few years.

Then, while we were using both languages, industry could make the changeover. (Actually, it would not be such a wrench. The electrical industry uses metric measurements when they use watts and kilowatts, as I shall explain later in the book, and it doesn't seem to mind.)

Thus, eventually, the common system could be dropped altogether, and we could join the rest of the world in a union of logical measurements.

COMPARING THE SYSTEMS

How does the metric system compare with ours in size of units? In other words, how long are metric units in the common units with which we are familiar?

Well, conversion factors can be set up to convert metric units into common units as easily as to convert versts into miles. And if any one conversion figure is given, all the rest can be calculated from the tables of common units of length and metric units of length already given in the book.

Suppose, for instance, actual measurement tells you that 1 hectometer = 328.08 feet. You can use that knowledge to prepare a conversion factor for turning dekameters into yards. Thus, since 1 hectometer = 10 dekameters, then 10 dekameters = 328.08 feet and 1 dekameter = 32.808 feet. Furthermore, since there are 3 feet in a yard, 1 dekameter = 32.808/3 or 10.936 yards and that is the conversion you wanted.

In this way, every conversion factor can be calculated and the metric units can be added to the table of common units. A combined table giving all conversion factors can easily be prepared. However, there is no need to be that complete. Hectometers and dekameters, for example, are rarely used and the conversion factors turning them into feet and yards are not important.

In fact, the metric units of length commonly used in everyday life are only three: the centimeter, the meter, and the kilometer. These are most often converted into the inch, yard, and miles respectively. The necessary conversion factors are:

1 kilometer = 0.621372 mile (3280.8 feet)
1 mile = 1.60935 kilometers

1 meter	= 1.093611	yards (39.3700 inches)
1 yard	= 0.914402	meter
1 centimeter	= 0.39370	inch
1 inch	= 2.540005	centimeters

(For day-to-day work, of course, it isn't necessary to use the conversion factors in full—in this case or in any other. Except where great accuracy is needed, it is enough, for instance, to set a kilometer equal to 5/8 of a mile, a meter to 1 1/10 yards, and a centimeter to 2/5 of an inch.)

The conversion factors given above, by the way, are for American units of length. The United States does not have a "standard yard." Like most other nations it has a standard meter. The American meter is called the *United States Prototype Meter 27*. This is a platinum-iridium bar kept under strict guard in an air-conditioned vault in Washington. The American yard was defined as exactly 3600/3937 of this standard meter. In this way, although the United States does not use the metric system, its measures are pegged to that system.

The British, however, do have a standard yard, the *British Imperial Yard*. It is a bronze bar manufactured in 1844. The tradition-minded British will not switch to platinum-iridium and their standard, of the more changeable bronze, seems to have shrunk a very tiny bit since 1844. The most recent measurement makes the British Imperial Yard equal to 3,600,000/3,937,014 meters.

This means that the British Imperial Yard is very slightly shorter than the American yard. Naturally, all the other units of length used by the British, based on their yard, are correspondingly smaller than the equivalent American units based on their yard.

The British inch, for instance, is equal to 2.539998 centimeters, while the American inch is, as listed above, equal to 2.540005 centimeters. (The equivalent difference between the British mile and the American mile comes to about 1/30 of an inch.) These are small differences but they show up in extremely refined measurements.

There is, however, an *international inch* in which the difference is split. The international inch is set equal to exactly 2.540000 centimeters. This is the inch used in Canada, so it might be called the *Canadian inch*.

In 1959, the English-speaking nations assembled in conference and agreed to switch to the international inch beginning the first of July of that year. Under that system, the standard yard in all the English-speaking countries is 3,600,000/3,937,008 meters.

Thank goodness for at least that microscopic movement in the direction of common sense!

Acres and Gallons

SQUARING AND CUBING THE UNITS

I have mentioned that distances can be added and subtracted in the same manner as numbers alone, provided that units are made equivalent. Thus, 5 feet plus 3 feet equals 8 feet, while 5 feet minus 3 feet equals 2 feet.

What about multiplication, though? What about 5 feet times 3 feet?

Suppose, for instance, you have a small rectangular plot of ground 5 feet in one direction and 3 feet in the other. In order to obtain its *area* (that is, the amount of ground it covers), its length must be multiplied by its width. The result is 15 something-or-other and if you look at the accompanying diagram you will see that the plot can indeed be broken up into 15 squares.

Each of the squares is a foot in each direction so such a square is said to be a *square foot* in area. Consequently, 5 feet × 3 feet = 15 square feet.

In the same way, suppose you had a box which was 5 feet in length by 2 feet in width by 3 feet in height. The *volume* (that is, the amount of space it contained, or took up) is the product of the length, width, and height. This amounts to 5 feet × 3 feet × 2 feet, or 30 something-or-

SQUARES AND CUBES

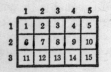

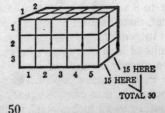

15 HERE
15 HERE
TOTAL 30

other. Sure enough, the box can be broken up into 30 cubes, each cube a foot on each side. Such a cube is a *cubic foot,* so 5 feet × 3 feet × 2 feet = 30 cubic feet.

Just as the foot is a unit of length, the square foot is a unit of area and the cubic foot is a unit of volume.

If your rectangles and boxes had been measured in inches, the answers would have come out in square inches and cubic inches. If they had been measured in yards, the answers would have come out in square yards and cubic yards, and so on.

Naturally, the multiplications are not performed until the units are made the same. To multiply 2 yards by 3 feet, you must first convert 2 yards to 6 feet, or 3 feet to 1 yard. In the former case, the problem becomes 6 feet × 3 feet = 18 square feet; while in the latter case it becomes 2 yards × 1 yard = 2 square yards.

Since the answer must be the same in either case, that means that 2 square yards is the same as 18 square feet. We can show that this is so in another way. We know that 1 yard is equal to 3 feet. Then 1 square yard, which is equal

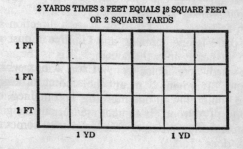

2 YARDS TIMES 3 FEET EQUALS 18 SQUARE FEET
OR 2 SQUARE YARDS

1 FT

1 FT

1 FT

1 YD   1 YD

to 1 yard × 1 yard, must also be equal to 3 feet × 3 feet, or to 9 square feet. If 1 square yard is equal to 9 square feet, then 2 square yards is indeed equal to 18 square feet.

In general, we can easily set up conversion factors for units of area and units of volume from the units of length we already have.

Pick any conversion factor at random; say 1 foot = 12 inches. In that case, 1 square foot is equal to 1 foot × 1 foot, or to 12 inches × 12 inches, or to 144 square inches.

In the same way, 1 cubic foot is equal to 1 foot × 1 foot × 1 foot, or 12 inches × 12 inches × 12 inches, or 1728 cubic inches.

Do you see that 144 is the square of 12 (that is, 12 × 12) and that 1728 is the cube of 12 (that is 12 × 12 × 12)? In general, when different units of length are squared into units of area, the conversion factor connecting them is also squared. In cubing the lengths into units of volume, the conversion factors are cubed.

The *square mile* is the most familiar unit of area since it is used in measuring the areas of states and nations. Square feet and square yards may be used in measuring floor areas, and square inches in measuring television screens. By and large, though, if the average man is hazy on the conversion factors for the common units of length, he is more confused still on the conversion factors for the common units of area. Not one person in a hundred, probably, can say offhand how many square inches there are in a square foot, or how many square feet in a square yard. I won't even mention the other conversion factors, or the fact that surveyors use such units of area as *square chains* and *square links,* which involve even less well-known conversion factors.

Yet there is one common and familiar unit of area that doesn't fit neatly into the scheme. This is the *acre*.

The word "acre" come from a Latin word meaning "pasture land." It originally meant the amount of land a yoke of oxen could plow in one morning, and this was set equal to 4 *roods.* (A "rood" is another measure that gets its name from a measuring stick since the word comes from the same root as does "rod.")

Measuring your land in roods and acres was therefore a good and practical idea. It told you the time you might expect to use up in getting your land plowed. The only trouble is that the amount you can plow depends not only on the size of your plot, but also on its hilliness or rockiness and on the strength of your oxen. So acres tended to vary in size from place to place.

Various English kings set the acre equal to a rectangle of land 40 rods long by 4 rods wide. That was apparently judged the average morning's plowing job. A rectangle 40 rods by 4 rods has an area of 40 × 4 or 160 square rods. Consequently, an acre is now officially 160 square rods. Since a square rod is 5½ × 5½ or 30¼ square yards, an acre is equal to 160 × 30¼ or 4840 square yards. (A rood, which is still used in England and Scotland, though not in the United States, is a quarter of an acre. It is therefore equal to 40 square rods, or 1210 square yards in area.)

Since a square furlong contains 1600 square rods, while an acre contains only 160 square rods, you can see that 1 square furlong = 10 acres. Again, since 1 square mile contains 64 square furlongs, it must contain 64 × 10 or 640 acres. In other words:

$$1 \text{ square mile} = 640 \text{ acres}$$
$$1 \text{ acre} = 4 \text{ roods}$$
$$1 \text{ rood} = 40 \text{ square rods}$$

As for the units of volume obtained by cubing units of length, these are even less well known than the units of area. About the only use such measures have in ordinary life is in the expression of the size of refrigerators or freezers in cubic feet.

However, some dealers in bulky objects still use old-fashioned units of volume that are based on multiples of the cubic foot. For instance, dealers in wood use the *cord* (so-called because such a quantity of wood was bound into a bundle by a line or cord). A cord of wood is supposed to make up a bundle 8 feet long by 4 feet wide and 4 feet high. This comes to 8 × 4 × 4, or 128 cubic feet. A one-foot length of such a bundle would be 1 × 4 × 4, or 16 cubic feet, and this is a *cord foot*.

In dealing with stonework and masonry, use is made of the *perch* as a unit of volume. ("Perch" is another old word for a measuring rod.) This is most commonly set equal to a pile that is 16½ feet long, 1 foot wide, and 1½ feet high, which comes out to 24¾ cubic feet. (I have a notion that the odd measurements arose because, in early times, the mason measured the pile of rock as being 1 rod long, 1 foot wide, and 1 cubit high.)

Anyway, to summarize:

1 cord foot	=	16	cubic feet
1 perch	=	24¾	cubic feet
1 cord	=	128	cubic feet (8 cord feet)

METRIC SIMPLICITY AGAIN

How is the situation in the metric system in comparison? Since the units of length increase by factors of 10, the corresponding units of area must increase by factors of 10×10, or 100; and the corresponding units of volume increase by factors of $10 \times 10 \times 10$, or 1000.

Thus, for the metric units of area:

1 square kilometer	=	100 square hectometers
1 square hectometer	=	100 square dekameters

And for the metric units of volunme:

1 cubic kilometer	=	1000 cubic hectometers
1 cubic hectometer	=	1000 cubic dekameters

and so on. What could be simpler?

There are a couple of special names for some of these metric units. It is my personal opinion that special names detract from the beautiful symmetry and logic of the metric system. However, they are adopted to save breath. For instance, the commonly used unit of area, the square dekameter, is also called the *are* (from the same root as "area"). The are, pronounced "ahr," is a word of three letters and one syllable, as compared with the 15 letters and 5 syllables, in English, of "square dekameter."

The most common metric unit used to measure the area of farms and similar plots of ground is the *hectare*. This is equal, as the prefix implies, to 100 ares; that is, to a square hectometer.

Among the units of volume, the cubic meter is commonly called a *stere,* from a Greek word meaning "solid."

The conversion of units of area and volume from the common system to the metric system, and vice versa, involves squaring and cubing the ordinary conversion factors for the units of length.

For instance, 1 inch is equal to 2.54 centimeters. Therefore, 1 square inch is equal to 2.54 × 2.54, or 6.45 square centimeters. Similarly, 1 cubic inch is equal to 2.54 × 2.54 × 2.54, or 16.39 cubic centimeters.

Again, since the meter is equal to about 1.094 yards, the square meter is equal to 1.094 × 1.094, or 1.196 square yards. The cubic meter (stere) is equal to 1.094 × 1.094 × 1.094, or 1.308 cubic yards.

One particularly useful conversion among units of area is that between hectares and acres. Since a hectare is equal to a square hectometer, it is equal to 100 × 100, or 10,000 square meters. (A square meter, by the way, is equal to 1/100 square dekameters, or, in other words, 1/100 are. For that reason, a square meter is sometimes called a *centare.*)

Since a square meter equals 1.196 square yards, a hectare equals 10,000 × 1.196, or 11,960 square yards. But an acre is equal to 4840 square yards, as I explained in the previous section. Therefore, 1 hectare is equal to 11,960/4840 or:

$$1 \text{ hectare} = 2.471 \text{ acres}$$
$$1 \text{ acre} = 0.405 \text{ hectare}$$

THE CONFUSION OF VOLUME

One of the reasons why cubic units are not often used as measures of volume in the English-speaking countries is that there are traditional units of volume that compete with them. These other units have no connection with the common units of length, but arose in other ways.

For instance, there is *liquid measure,* a collection of units which are used to measure the volume of liquids such as water, milk, oil, vinegar, and wine. I am going to include a rather long list of such units, most of which you won't recognize, because I want to show how complicated the common measures are and how little is known of them. Here they are:

1 tun	=	2 pipes
1 pipe	=	2 hogsheads
1 hogshead	=	2 barrels
1 barrel	=	3½ firkins
1 firkin	=	9 gallons
1 gallon	=	4 liquid quarts
1 liquid quart	=	2 liquid pints
1 liquid pint	=	4 gills

The names of most of these units are old words of uncertain origin. *Quart* is from the Latin word meaning "four" since there are four of them to the gallon. The word *firkin* may also be a corruption of "four," since there are nearly four of them to the barrel.

Notice that in this table many of the conversion factors are 2 or 4, the latter being 2 × 2. This is a sign of a primitive table, since in early days the simplest way of dividing any measure was to halve it, or quarter it.

For everyday work, the gill is the smallest convenient measure. The only people who, before the days of modern science, were likely to work with smaller volumes were the apothecaries, who dealt with drugs. The *apothecaries' fluid measure*, therefore, extends down through smaller units than a gill, as follows:

1 gill	=	4 fluid ounces
1 fluid ounce	=	8 fluid drams
1 fluid dram	=	60 minims

I'll have occasion later on to explain the derivation of *ounce* and *dram*, but I can talk about the *minim* now. It comes from a Latin word meaning "least" since it was the smallest unit of volume the apothecaries could work with. It is about equal to a drop of liquid.

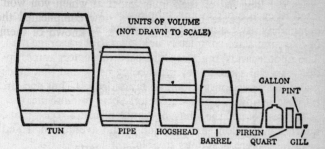

UNITS OF VOLUME
(NOT DRAWN TO SCALE)

GALLON
PINT

TUN   PIPE   HOGSHEAD   FIRKIN
BARREL   QUART   GILL

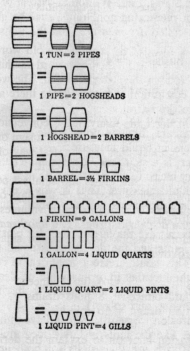

1 TUN = 2 PIPES

1 PIPE = 2 HOGSHEADS

1 HOGSHEAD = 2 BARRELS

1 BARREL = 3½ FIRKINS

1 FIRKIN = 9 GALLONS

1 GALLON = 4 LIQUID QUARTS

1 LIQUID QUART = 2 LIQUID PINTS

1 LIQUID PINT = 4 GILLS

As you see, all these units of volume are not related to units of length in any simple way. They are not even related to each other in any simple way. We're stuck with a completely useless mess, and the proof of that is that most of these units are completely unknown to the average man. The apothecaries' units are still used in doctors' prescriptions, special symbols for them being used, and that helps make the prescriptions look so mysterious. (That and the horrible handwriting which doctors seem to cultivate.)

In fact, of all the units of liquid measure, only pints, quarts, and gallons are familiar to the average man and even here there is serious trouble.

In the United States, there is another system of units of volume, used for measuring nonliquids, such as grain and vegetables. It is called *dry measure,* and the units follow:

$$1 \text{ bushel } = 4 \text{ pecks}$$
$$1 \text{ peck } = 8 \text{ dry quarts}$$
$$1 \text{ dry quart} = 2 \text{ dry pints}$$

Bushel and *peck* are old words of uncertain origin, but pints and quarts are familiar now. At least, we've just come across them in liquid measure.

That, however, is a snare and a delusion. The pint and quart used in dry measure are not the same as the pint and quart used in liquid measure. That is why I have differentiated them into dry pints and dry quarts, and liquid pints and liquid quarts.

The dry measures are the larger. The dry pint is equal to 1.164 liquid pints and the dry quart is equal to 1.164 liquid quarts. (This would create a great deal of confusion were it not for the fact that in ordinary life we deal almost exclusively with liquid pints and quarts in buying milk, beverages, ice cream, and so on.)

To make confusion worse, the British have units of volume with names like the units in liquid measure and dry measure. The British use their units for both liquid and dry and in that respect (for a change) have things less confused than the Americans do. The British table of units of volume is:

$$
\begin{array}{rcl}
1 \text{ bushel} & = & 4 \text{ pecks} \\
1 \text{ peck} & = & 2 \text{ gallons} \\
1 \text{ gallon} & = & 4 \text{ quarts} \\
1 \text{ quart} & = & 2 \text{ pints} \\
1 \text{ pint} & = & 4 \text{ gills} \\
1 \text{ gill} & = & 5 \text{ fluid ounces}
\end{array}
$$

If the fluid ounce were the same in both nations, the British gill would be 5/4 or 1.25 times the American gill. However, the British fluid ounce is somewhat smaller than the American:

$$
\begin{array}{rcl}
1 \text{ British fluid ounce} & = & 0.961 \text{ American fluid ounce} \\
1 \text{ American fluid ounce} & = & 1.041 \text{ British fluid ounces}
\end{array}
$$

The British gill, therefore, is 1.25×0.961, or 1.201 times as large as an American gill. This means:

$$
\begin{array}{rcl}
1 \text{ British gill} & = & 1.201 \text{ American gills} \\
1 \text{ American gill} & = & 0.833 \text{ British gill}
\end{array}
$$

The pint is made up of four gills in both systems, and the quart of two pints. The difference in the gills carries over into the pints and quarts. The British pint and quart are 1.201 times as large in volume as the American liquid pint and liquid quart.

The British gallon, called the *British Imperial Gallon*, is equal to 1.201 American gallons. It is the British Imperial Gallon that is the measure used in Canada, so if you travel across the border and ask to have your gas tank filled, you may be surprised to find that your tank doesn't hold as much gasoline as you always thought it did. If your tank has a 17-gallon capacity, for instance, it will only hold 17/1.2 or just a trifle over 14 Canadian gallons.

Similarly, at least one beverage company advertises that its bottles hold an "imperial quart," meaning a British quart. That, naturally, will mean one additional glassful.

In the same conference that split the difference between the American inch and the British inch, some effort was made to establish an "international gallon." The difference, however, between the British Imperial Gallon and the American gallon was too great, and no agreement could be reached.

The British pint and quart are also slightly larger than

THE DIFFERENT QUARTS

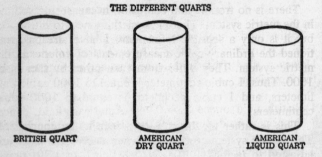

BRITISH QUART   AMERICAN   AMERICAN
                       DRY QUART   LIQUID QUART

the American dry pint and dry quart. The British pint (or quart), as we have noted, is equal to 1.201 times the American liquid pint (or liquid quart), while the American dry pint (or dry quart) is equal to 1.164 times the American liquid pint (or liquid quart). From this we can see that the British pint (or quart) must be equal to 1.201/ 1.164 times the American dry pint (or dry quarts). Consequently:

1 British pint   = 1.032 American dry pints
  (or quart)   (or dry quarts)
1 American dry pint   = 0.969 British pint
  (or dry quart)   (or quart)

Since the British pecks and bushels are built up out of British quarts and the American pecks and bushels out of American dry quarts, it turns out that the British peck is equal to 1.032 times the American peck and the British bushel is equal to 1.032 times the American bushel.

Thus, the English-speaking countries increase the complications of their measures. Indeed, they are blessed with three different pints and three different quarts.

If you are confused about all these units of volume, believe me, so am I. In fact, I get furious every time I try to make sense out of them. It is a relief to turn to the metric system again.

REFINING THE METRIC VOLUMES

There is no trouble and confusion in measuring volume in the metric system. There is something new to introduce, but it is only a sensible refinement. I have already mentioned the ordinary cubic measurements of volume in the metric system. They differ from each other by factors of 1000. Thus, 1 cubic centimeter is equal to 1000 cubic millimeters, and 1 cubic decimeter is equal to 1000 cubic centimeters.

This is rather too large a difference to be convenient. The metric system works best when successive units are adjusted to factors of 10.

In order to do this for units of volume, a cubic measure of convenient size for everyday use was chosen. This was the cubic decimeter. It was given a new name, the *liter* (or *litre,* in French, from the name of an old French measure of similar size).

(Actually, through a slight error which I'll talk about further in the next chapter, the liter is not quite exactly one cubic decimeter in volume. This is one of the few imperfections in the metric system, but the error is so slight as not to be noticeable in any but the most delicate measurements. We will be only slightly wrong to say that 1 liter = 1 cubic decimeter.)

The liter can be subdivided by units of ten or built up by units of ten, using the same prefixes which were used in the original units of length. Thus:

1 kiloliter	= 10 hectoliters	=	1 cubic meter
1 hectoliter	= 10 dekaliters	= 100	cubic decimeters
1 dekaliter	= 10 liters	= 10	cubic decimeters
1 liter	= 10 deciliters	= 1	cubic decimeter
1 deciliter	= 10 centiliters	= 100	cubic centimeters
1 centiliter	= 10 milliliters	= 10	cubic centimeters
1 milliliter		= 1	cubic centimeter

Here again the advantages of the metric system shine out. Please note well that one set of prefixes is used in all metric measurements. Once you have memorized the fact that a decimeter is a tenth of a meter, you know that a deciliter is a tenth of a liter and that a deci-anything, in fact, is a tenth of an anything.

You see, I suppose, why the liter is more useful than the cubic decimeter. The next higher unit on the cubic scale is the cubic meter, which is 1000 cubic decimeters. In between those two cubic units, however, are the dekaliter and the hectoliter. Similarly, the unit on the cubic scale which is next below the cubic decimeter is the cubic centimeter, which is 1/1000 as large. And between these two cubic units, are the deciliter and the centiliter.

The two particular units in the liter system which are most commonly used are the liter itself and the milliliter. The liter is between the liquid quart and the dry quart in size:

1 liter = 1.0567 American liquid quarts
1 liter = 0.9081 American dry quart

To work it the other way:

1 American liquid quart = 0.9463 liter
1 American dry quart = 1.1012 liters

Ounces and Grams

THE MEASURE OF MASS

So far I have talked only about units of length, area, and volume. Area, however, was obtained by multiplying two units of length, and volume by multiplying three units of length. Consequently, it all boils down to units of length after all. This is reasonable, though, because the first measure mankind learned to handle, probably, was that of length.

There is another type of measure that is also very ancient and that is the measure of *mass*. (Actually, the average man, in speaking of mass, usually calls it *weight*. But mass and weight are different, even though this difference doesn't show up under ordinary conditions. I will explain the difference later and meanwhile I will keep referring to "mass" even where you might feel it more natural and proper to say "weight.")

Small objects of irregular shape, such as lumps of metal, could be compared in size by measuring the volume taken up by each. However, it is not easy to measure the volume of irregularly shaped objects. It wasn't until about 250 B.C. that the Greek scientist Archimedes of Syracuse discovered how to do it. The necessities of life could not wait for an Archimedes to be born, and thousands of years before his time, men were comparing the size of objects by measuring their masses.

This was most easily done by means of the *beam scale,* an invention that is older than the Pyramids. Most of us are familiar with it. (Cartoonists often depict Justice as a goddess with a bandage over her eyes and a beam scale in her hand.)

The beam scale consists of a horizontal rod, called the

beam, which is suspended at its center. From each end of the beam is suspended a *pan*. When the pans are empty, they remain level. If an object is placed in one pan, the pan moves down; the other empty pan moves up. If an object is placed in each pan, the pan that contains the more massive object moves down; the one that contains the less massive object moves up. If the pans remain level, the two objects are of equal mass.

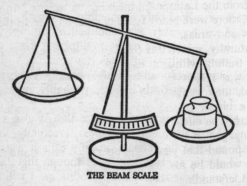

THE BEAM SCALE

But suppose you have two small lumps of gold which are nearly alike. If you put them into the pans of a balance, you can tell which is the more massive. Ah, but by how much is the more massive one more massive?

Well, put one lump of gold on one pan of the scale. On the other pan, start adding a series of objects against which you might compare the mass of the gold. The objects might be dried grains of some cereal such as wheat or barley. These are handy about a farm and can be chosen so as to be nearly alike in size and shape, therefore nearly alike in mass.

Suppose, doing this, you find that you must add fourteen grains before the pans balance. Now empty the pans and put the second bit of gold in the first pan. Start adding the grains again to the other pan, and you may find that it now takes fifteen grains to balance the scales.

Your conclusion is that the first bit of gold is 14 grains in mass, the second 15 grains. The second bit is more massive by 1 grain.

Modern scientists use balances that are just like the original beam scale in principle, but are much more delicate and elaborate. And among the units of mass used in the English-speaking countries, there is still one called the *grain*.

As time passed, each nation and region developed its own standard masses against which unknown masses could be compared. The chief such unit is called *pound* in English, from the Latin word meaning "a weight." In medieval times, there were many types of pounds used in the various towns and areas.

Naturally, merchants from outside some local area who were trading within it had to have it clearly understood what was meant by a "pound." If they charged by the pound, they wanted to be certain the customer didn't expect a bigger pound than the merchant counted on delivering. The customer was interested, too. In fact, all people engaged in trade and commerce were anxious to use some pound that was well supervised and standardized so there would be as little chance as possible to suffer from misunderstandings.

The first pound to be accepted throughout England was the *Troy pound* and one story is that the pound derives its name from the city of Troyes in France. Troyes was a prosperous trading center in the Middle Ages, well known for the annual fairs that were held there. Merchants traveled considerable distances to attend those fairs and it was to the advantage of Troyes to encourage their attendance by establishing good, well-supervised measures.

Perhaps, then, it was the pound of Troyes that was accepted in England in the 1200's as the Troy pound. This pound (although not our common pound of today) is still used in the United States as a measure of such items as gold, silver, and jewels.

THE VALUE OF TWELVE

The Troy pound is divided into 12 *Troy ounces*. The word "ounce" (like the word "inch") comes from a Latin word meaning "a twelfth," which is natural since the ounce is a twelfth of this pound.

Twelve is a convenient small number into which to divide a unit, more convenient than ten for people who are not at ease with fractions. After all, 12 can be divided evenly by 2, 3, 4, and 6, while 10 can be divided evenly only by 2 and 5. The factor 12 hangs on in modern times not only in the inch and the ounce, but in the fact that there are 24 hours (2×12) in a day, 12 objects in a dozen, and 12 dozen in a gross. There will be other examples shortly.

For instance, the table of Troy units of mass is as follows:

1 Troy pound = 12 Troy ounces
1 Troy ounce = 20 pennyweights
1 pennyweight = 24 grains

The grain, as I said earlier, recalls the dim old days when grains of cereal were used as small units of mass. The *pennyweight* derives its name from the fact that a silver penny coined in England in the Middle Ages was just 24 grains in mass. Hence, a pennyweight was literally the "weight of a penny." (Notice that 24 is 2×12; the number 12 shows up again.)

In fact, English coinage still follows the Troy unit of mass. To this day, 12 English pennies make an English shilling and 20 shillings make an English pound. This means there are 240 pennies to the pound, so that a pound of money was, at one time, literally a pound; a Troy pound of silver.

A well-organized system such as the Troy units of mass was used particularly for precious objects where a small error might mean an important loss. So Troy measure was used for gold and silver and is still so used. In fact, the most familiar word in connection with gold, to the average man of today, is the *carat* and that, too, originated as a Troy unit of mass.

The word "carat" is thought to be derived from an Arabic word for a kind of bean. So this, like "grain," is a unit of mass based on a plant product. The medieval goldsmiths are supposed to have set one carat equal to 12 grains. (There's 12 again.) That would make the carat equal to half of a pennyweight. An old coin called the *mark* had a mass of 24 carats (or 12 pennyweights; 12 still again). Such a coin wasn't pure gold, because pure gold is too soft to make coins with. Other metals, such as copper, had to be added to harden it.

Naturally, it would be easy for goldsmiths to cheat the people by putting a little too much copper into the coins. Consequently, there had to be regulations governing the quantity of gold in the coins. If each 24-carat gold mark contained, say 22 carats of gold, it was "22-carat gold" and had to be marked so. Or it might be "18-carat gold" or "14-carat gold." Naturally there would be severe penalties for mismarking the gold to be used for coins.

This hangs on to this day. Any gold object, regardless of its total mass, is marked "14-carat" if it is 14/24 gold, or "18-carat" if it is 18/24 gold, and so on.

Unfortunately, confusion arises because there is another and smaller carat that is used for jewels, particularly for diamonds. This smaller carat was intended originally to be 4 grains in mass (which would make it 1/3 the mass of the goldsmith's carat). However, different areas of Europe had carats of different size and the English carat, used in the London diamond market, ended up being equal to 3.163 grains. But this is still not exactly the carat used for jewels today, and I will leave a further discussion of it for later in the chapter.

Like gold and silver, drugs and medicines must be handled in small quantities and very accurately. Apothecaries, like goldsmiths and silversmiths, therefore used the Troy measure. For that reason, the Troy pound and Troy ounce are sometimes called the *apothecaries' pound* and *apothecaries' ounce*. For masses less than an ounce, apothecaries used units that were not quite like the usual Troy units, so that we can prepare a table of apothecary units of mass as follows:

1 apothecaries' pound = 12 apothecaries' ounces
   (Troy pound)   (Troy ounces)

1 apothecaries' ounce	=	8 apothecaries' drams
(Troy ounce)		
1 apothecaries' dram	=	3 scruples
1 scruple		= 20 grains

The *scruple* comes from a Latin word meaning "small stone" and this harks back to a time when pebbles may have been used as standard masses. The *dram* comes from the Greek coin "drachma" and probably originated as the weight of one of those coins, just as the pennyweight is the weight of a penny. The British, in fact, spell the unit as *drachm*. I call it the "apothecaries' dram" here to distinguish it from the "fluid dram" which the apothecaries also use, but as a unit of volume.

Since a scruple is 20 grains, whereas a pennyweight is 24 grains, a scruple is 20/24 or:

1 scruple	= 0.833 pennyweight
1 pennyweight	= 1.2 scruples

Similarly, an apothecaries' dram is 20×3, or 60 grains and (60 is equal to 5×12, if you're still watching for twelves). Consequently, an apothecaries' dram is 60/24 the mass of a pennyweight or:

1 apothecaries' dram	= 2.5 pennyweights
1 pennyweight	= 0.4 apothecaries' dram

Notice, too, that the number of scruples in an apothecaries' ounce is 3×8, or 24. This is 2×12. Truly, 12 shows up nearly everywhere in the older units of mass.

THE NEW POUND

Both Troy units and apothecary units have been overshadowed, in the English-speaking countries, by still a third system, the *avoirdupois* unit of mass. The word "avoirdupois" comes from medieval French words meaning "goods of weight," because it was used for goods that were dealt with in considerable quantity and not in the petty amounts that precious metals, jewels, and drugs were.

The avoirdupois units might not have been as carefully controlled originally as were the Troy units. Therefore, the avoirdupois weights were cheaper to make and easier to obtain. After all, to deal with wood and grain by wagon-loads, one didn't need the finicking accuracy that gold-smiths demanded.

By the 1500's avoirdupois units were more generally used in England than Troy units. Then, of course, people would naturally demand accuracy, and by now the avoir-dupois standards are as accurate as (or more so than) the Troy standards.

Some of the avoirdupois units are as follows:

1 avoirdupois pound = 16 avoirdupois ounces
1 avoirdupois ounce = 16 avoirdupois drams
1 avoirdupois dram = 27 11/32 grains

POUNDS AND OUNCES

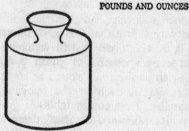

AVOIRDUPOIS POUND   TROY POUND

AVOIRDUPOIS OUNCE   TROY OUNCE

All these units have familiar names—pound, ounce, dram, and grain. Of them all, though, only the grain is the same unit as is found in the Troy apothecary tables. The *avoirdupois dram* with 27 11/32 grains is not the same as the apothecaries' dram, containing 60 grains. The apoth-ecaries' dram is over twice as large. In fact:

1 apothecaries' dram = 2.194 avoirdupois drams
1 avoirdupois dram = 0.456 apothecaries' dram

Nor are the ounces the same. The *avoirdupois ounce* contains 27 11/32 × 16 or 437 1/2 grains, while the Troy ounce is slightly larger, 24 × 20 or 480 grains. Therefore, the Troy ounce is equal to 480/437 1/2 or:

1 Troy ounce   = 1.097 avoirdupois ounces
1 avoirdupois ounce = 0.911 Troy ounce

Notice, too, that although the avoirdupois ounce derives its name from the Latin meaning "one twelfth," it is one sixteenth of an avoirdupois pound. The name fits the Troy unit but not the avoirdupois unit. Why sixteen? Remember that the simplest way of dividing any unit is to halve it. Then you can halve each half to get quarters; halve each quarter to get eighths; halve each eighth to get sixteenths. There are your sixteenths.

The avoirdupois ounce was once equal in mass to the Troy ounce (which is why it is called "ounce") but was deliberately cut down in mass in order that the avoirdupois pound might come out an even number of grains. As it is, the number of grains in an avoirdupois pound is 16 times the 437 1/2 grains present in each of the avoirdupois ounces the pound contains. That comes to 7000 grains. Had the avoirdupois ounce remained the size of the Troy ounce, the number of grains in the avoirdupois pound would have been 16 × 480, or 7680 grains.

The Troy pound, on the other hand, is made up of 12 Troy ounces so that it contains 480 × 12, or 5760 grains. The avoirdupois pound is therefore the greater.

1 avoirdupois pound = 1.215 Troy pounds
1 Troy pound   = 0.823 avoirdupois pound

Of course, the cutting down of the mass of the avoirdupois ounce meant the cutting down of the mass of the avoirdupois dram (so that there might remain the convenient number of 16 drams to the ounce). The grain, as the basic unit, was not changed. After all, the Troy units and the apothecary units also depend upon it. That is why the avoirdupois dram ended with the curiously uneven content of 27 11/32 grains.

All these various drams, ounces, and pounds are typical of the usual confusion in the measures used in the English-speaking world. What makes it not so bad as it might be, is that only the avoirdupois units are commonly used. When an "ounce" or "pound" is mentioned, without any indication as to the system it belongs to, it is always taken for granted that the avoirdupois system is intended.

The avoirdupois units of mass, since they are meant to measure the mass of bulky objects, include units of greater mass than a pound. For instance, in American usage:

1 ton = 20 hundredweights
1 hundredweight = 100 avoirdupois pounds

The *hundredweight* is self-explanatory, and the derivation of the word *ton* I will explain later.

In British usage, the avoirdupois units rise above the pound in somewhat different fashion:

1 ton = 20 hundredweights
1 hundredweight = 4 quarters
1 quarter = 2 stones
1 stone = 14 avoirdupois pounds

The *quarter* is clearly named because it is a quarter of a hundredweight. The *stone* (like scruple) harks back to the time when stones were used as units of mass. The reason why a stone should be 14 avoirdupois pounds in mass is not clear to me. Since the British are involved, I should say "tradition" is a sufficient answer. Certainly, 14 is an inconvenient number and, offhand, I can't think of any other unit that goes into a larger unit 14 times.

The existence of the number 14 confuses things badly. The *British hundredweight* is equal to $14 \times 2 \times 4$, or 112 avoirdupois pounds. It seems illogical to call 112 avoirdupois pounds a "hundredweight" but the British do it.

The Americans inherited this but were not quite as satisfied as the British seem to be to sacrifice logic to tradition. The Americans eliminated the stone and made the hundredweight a true hundredweight.

This discrepancy shows up in the ton also. Both British and American tons are made up of 20 hundredweights. The British ton, however, consists of 20 British hundredweights, which comes to 112×20, or 2240 avoirdupois pounds. The American ton consists of 20 American hundredweights, which comes to 100×20, or 2000 pounds. Thus:

$$1 \text{ British ton } = 1.12 \text{ American tons}$$
$$1 \text{ American ton} = 0.984 \text{ British ton}$$

In common speech, the British ton is often called a *long ton* or a *gross ton,* while the American ton is the *short ton* or *net ton.* In the same way there is the *long hundredweight* or *gross hundredweight* for the British variety, and the *short hundredweight* or *net hundredweight* for the American.

(Americans are most aware of the British units of mass when they read British novels and find that some character is referred to as "a husky athlete of fourteen stone" or "a mere slip of a girl of barely seven stone." Generally, the American reader shrugs his shoulders and keeps on reading.)

MASS AND VOLUME

Units of length probably appeared first in human history, then units of mass. When units of volume finally arose, they were not based upon units of length (as is most logical from the mathematical standpoint) but on units of mass. The latter was less logical, perhaps, but more practical for people without much mathematical background.

Thus, the British Imperial Gallon is that volume which will hold 10 avoirdupois pounds of water. Do you see how easy it is to check such a gallon measure? A liquid (and water is the most easily available) will take on the shape of any container and fill it without leaving holes or spaces. Measure out a mass of 10 avoirdupois pounds of water, then, and pour it into the gallon container. If it all goes in, the gallon is honest. If any spills over, the gallon is short measure.

WHEN MASS EQUALS VOLUME

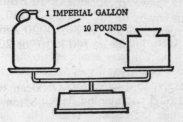

1 IMPERIAL GALLON
10 POUNDS

An American gallon, which is about 5/6 the size of the British Imperial Gallon, contains only 8.337 pounds of water. From this standpoint, the British Imperial Gallon is the more logical unit.

There are 8 pints to the gallon in both the American and the British systems. The British pint will hold 10/8 or 1.25 avoirdupois pounds of water. The American liquid pint will hold 8.337/8 or 1.042 avoirdupois pounds of water.

There is an old saying: "A pint's a pound the whole world round." As you see, this is almost true of the American liquid pint, at any rate.

Since the liquid pint is made up of 16 fluid ounces and the avoirdupois pound is made up of 16 avoirdupois ounces of water, the fluid ounce will hold 1.042 avoirdupois ounces of water. The fluid ounce will also hold 0.950 of the slightly larger Troy ounce of water. In fact, the "fluid ounce" undoubtedly gets its name from the fact that the mass of water it hold lies between the two common ounces of mass, the Troy ounce and the avoirdupois ounce.

In the same way a fluid dram (in the apothecaries' fluid measure) gets its name from the fact that it holds a quantity of water about equal in mass to one apothecaries' dram.

Another interesting connection between weight and volume involves the tun, which I listed as the largest unit in the table of liquid measure on page 56. It holds 252 gallons. If these are considered American gallons, the total mass of a tun of water is 252×8.337, or 2101 pounds. This is slightly over an American ton and, in fact, the word "ton" is thought to be derived from "tun." The connection is even closer if you remember that the tun often held wine rather than water and that wine is somewhat lighter than water.

An ancient unit of mass, familiar to us from the Bible, also arose out of volume. A *talent* (from a Greek word meaning "a weight") was supposed to have been, originally, the mass of a quantity of water, roughly equal, in our own measure, to a cubic foot. A cubic foot of water has a mass of 62.5 pounds, but the Greek talent was only 57 pounds, while the Hebrew talent (the one mentioned in the Bible) was about 94 pounds.

Since silver could be weighed by the talent, the talent also came to be a unit of money, just as the pound did. In modern terms, a Greek talent of silver might be worth $1800, while a Hebrew talent was worth about $3000.

Another Hebrew coin, the *shekel* (so familiar to us that it is even used as a slang term for money), was 1/3000 of a Hebrew talent and is therefore just about equivalent to the American dollar.

METRIC MASS

The metric system also ties volume to mass but, as you might expect, in a very logical and systematic way.

Thus, the mass of water contained in 1 milliliter, under certain specified conditions, was set equal to exactly 1 *gram.* (The word "gram" comes from an old Greek name for a small unit of mass.)

The gram is built up and divided down by tens, just as the liter and the meter are. There are thus a *dekagram, hectogram,* and *kilogram* working upward, and a *decigram, centigram,* and *milligram* working downward.

The metric system, then, combines not only its units of weight and volume (as the Anglo-American common system does, in a rather poor way), but combines both with the cubic units. For instance, a cubic centimeter, which is a cubic unit of length, is equal to a milliliter, which is a unit of volume, which holds a gram of water, which is a unit of mass.

Since a liter is equal to 1000 milliliters and a kilogram to 1000 grams, it follows that if a milliliter holds a gram of water, a liter holds a kilogram. Nearly a century ago, a mass of platinum-iridium was prepared that was just equal to the mass of water contained in a liter. This was called the *International Prototype Kilogram* and is now kept at Sèvres and serves as the primary standard of mass for all the world.

However, in 1927 the mass of water in a liter was measured by more delicate instruments than before. The mass was found to be the merest trifle less than what had been agreed upon as the standard kilogram. Scientists were therefore faced with two choices. They could adjust the standard kilogram, making it slightly smaller so that it really represented the mass of water in a liter. Or they could make the liter slightly larger so that it would hold a mass of water equal to the standard kilogram.

They decided that the second alternative would make less trouble and enlarged the liter. For that reason, the liter is now ever so slightly larger than the cubic decimeter and the milliliter just as slightly larger than the cubic centimeter. The conversion factors now are:

$$1 \text{ liter} = 1.000028 \text{ cubic decimeters}$$
$$1 \text{ cubic decimeter} = 0.999972 \text{ liter}$$

This difference matters only in the most refined measurements. Even so, chemists have gotten into the habit of expressing volume as milliliters and avoiding the use of the cubic centimeter.

The three most commonly used metric units of weight in everyday life are the milligram, gram, and kilogram. The milligram (1/1000 gram) is a very tiny unit and is much smaller than even the grain. The gram itself is still small, being considerably less than an avoirdupois ounce. The kilogram (1000 grams) is fairly large, however, quite a bit larger than an avoirdupois pound.

The conversion figures follow:

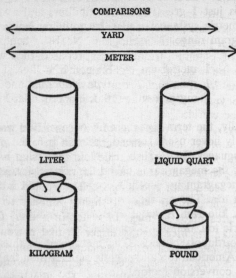

COMPARISONS

←————————————————————→ YARD

←————————————————————————→ METER

LITER   LIQUID QUART

KILOGRAM   POUND

1 milligram	= 0.0154	grain
1 grain	= 64.80	milligrams
1 gram	= 0.0353	avoirdupois ounce
1 avoirdupois ounce	= 28.35	grams
1 kilogram	= 2.205	avoirdupois pounds
1 avoirdupois pound	= 0.4536	kilogram

These conversion figures make it possible for me to return to the carat. Earlier in this chapter, I said that the British carat was equal to 3.163 grains. In metric units, the British carat therefore equals 3.163 × 64.80, or 204.96 milligrams.

Since much of the trade in diamonds and jewels generally is centered in countries which accept the metric system (Holland, for instance), it proved convenient to set up a new carat that was equal to an even number of milligrams.

For that reason, the *metric carat* was set equal to exactly 200 milligrams. The metric carat is now used internationally and was adopted officially by the United States in 1913.

If you are so fortunate as to own a 5-carat diamond, it has a mass of 5×200, or 1000 milligrams. Its mass, in other words, is just 1 gram.

The metric system can also be used for masses above the kilogram range. Thus:

$$1 \text{ megagram} = 10 \text{ quintals}$$
$$1 \text{ quintal} = 10 \text{ myriagrams}$$
$$1 \text{ myriagram} = 10 \text{ kilograms}$$

Actually, the term "megagram" (one million grams) is practically never used. Instead, the unit is called *tonne* in most languages. In English, to avoid confusion with our own ton, the megagram is called the *metric ton*.

The megagram is so called because its mass is roughly that of a ton. The metric ton is equal to 1000 kilograms and each kilogram is equal to 2.205 avoirdupois pounds. The metric ton, therefore, has a mass of 1000×2.205, or 2205 avoirdupois pounds. The metric ton is thus larger than the American ton and slightly smaller than the British ton. The conversion factors are:

$$1 \text{ metric ton} = 1.1023 \text{ short tons (American)}$$
$$1 \text{ metric ton} = 0.9842 \text{ long ton (British)}$$
$$1 \text{ short ton} = 0.9072 \text{ metric ton}$$
$$1 \text{ long ton} = 1.0160 \text{ metric tons}$$

MORE ANGLO-AMERICAN DISAGREEMENT

The standard of mass used in the United States was at first the British standard. Later, the United States set up a standard Troy pound of its own. The first one was called *Troy Pound of the Mint,* and the second, *Troy Pound of the National Bureau of Standards.* The latter is still used as a standard for coinage purposes.

For a while, the American avoirdupois pound was based on the Troy Pound of the Mint. In 1893, however, the United States switched to the kilogram as the basic standard. A standard was obtained called the *United States Prototype Kilogram 20.* The avoirdupois pound is defined as just 0.4535924277 of the mass of that standard kilogram.

As in the case of units of length, Great Britain is conservative enough to stick to its own standard of mass. It has for this purpose the *British Imperial Pound,* which was made up in 1845.

Apparently, since the Americans broke away to their own standard, the British Imperial Pound has somehow lost a very small quantity of mass. It is now a trifle smaller than the American standard. The British Imperial Pound is equal to 0.45359234 kilograms.

The American avoirdupois pound is thus equal to 0.4535924277/45359234 British Imperial pounds. This works out to:

1 American avoirdupois pound = 1.000001 British Imperial pounds

1 British Imperial pound = 0.9999999 American avoirdupois pound

This is an even smaller difference than that which existed in the case of the British and American inches. The pound difference, too, was ironed out at the same conference that settled the inch difference. The American avoirdupois pound was slightly shaved to bring it into line with the British Imperial Pound.

6   6   6   6   6   6   6   6   6   6

Seconds and Per Seconds

THE MEASURE OF TIME

Now that I have discussed units of length and units of mass, there is one other type of measure equally ancient. That is the measure of time.

Fortunately, this is very easily handled (in comparison to the measures of length and mass) because all the civilized world agrees on the units and did agree even before the metric system was established.

The units of time have a natural standard based on a scientific phenomenon all men, however primitive, seem to recognize. That phenomenon is the rotation of the earth, the time of which is almost perfectly constant. One complete rotation with respect to the sun is the *day* and this is divided (since Egyptian and Sumerian times) into 24 *hours*.

The hour is divided into 60 *minutes* and the minute into 60 *seconds*. This is quite similar to the units of angular measure given on page 38. The reason for the similarity is that the Babylonians first measured small units of time by following the motion of the sun as it wheeled in a huge, imaginary circle across the sky. Measuring the circular movement in degrees, minutes, and seconds was converted to measuring time in hours, minutes, and seconds. The habit has lasted ever since.

$$1 \text{ day} = 24 \text{ hours}$$
$$1 \text{ hour} = 60 \text{ minutes}$$
$$1 \text{ minute} = 60 \text{ seconds}$$

This means that in one day there are $24 \times 60 \times 60$, or 86,400 seconds. That second can therefore be defined as 1/86,400 of a day.

To be sure, the length of the day is very slowly increasing as the earth's rotation slows. This change in the day is not important under ordinary circumstances, since its length only increases by about one second every 100,000 years. However, if scientists decided they need a more constant standard than the earth's rotation, they can find it in the atomic vibrations within molecules. They can always define a second as being equal to the time taken for a certain atom within a certain molecule to vibrate so many times. As far as we know, that will never change.

There is another heavenly motion that is used as the basis for a common and well-known unit of time. That is the motion of the earth about the sun. One complete turn from spring equinox to spring equinox is called the *tropical year*. The tropical year does not fit evenly with the day. The conversion figures are:

1 tropical year = 365.2422   days
1 day   = 0.002737937 tropical year

For lengths of time over a year, oddly enough, the decimal system has always been used, ever since ancient times. Thus, ten years equal a *decade,* ten decades (a hundred years) equal a *century,* and ten centuries (a thousand years) equal a *millennium.* Notice that the prefixes eventually used in the metric system, "dec-", "cent-," and "mill-" show up here, but for successively larger units instead of smaller ones.

For lengths of time less than a second, the decimal system is also used. Foot races and horse races are usually timed to the tenth of a second. Shorter periods of time are useful only to scientists and they apply the metric system of prefixes directly. For instance, it is common to call a thousandth of a second a *millisecond* and a millionth of a second (a thousandth of a millisecond) a *microsecond.*

The original committee that established the metric system never attempted to do anything with time measurement. They realized that the day and the year were fixed by the rotation of the earth and by its revolution about the sun. Nothing could be done with either. The repetition of day and night, and of the seasons, was too basic and fundamental to be tampered with, and these simply could not be fitted into the decimal system.

What's more, the length of the month and of the week was originally established by the repetition of the phases of the moon, and it is extremely difficult to tamper with this, too. The French politicians of the Revolution tried to make adjustments by having each month just thirty days long (with five special holidays at the end of the year, six holidays in a leap year) and divided each month into three "decades" of ten days. This was a small move in the direction of decimals, but it just could not be put over.

Still, it seems to me that the metric committee may have missed a chance in the case of the one set of units that is not based on astronomical motions. They might have done something about the subdivisions of the day. Suppose they had decided to divide the day into 10 "metric hours," each "metric hour" into 100 "metric minutes," and each "metric minute" into 100 "metric seconds."

In that case a "metric hour" would be equal to 2 hours 24 minutes of ordinary time. A "metric minute" would be equal to 1 minute 26.4 seconds of ordinary time. A "metric second" would be equal to 0.864 ordinary seconds.

How much simpler it would be to handle these never-established units of time. In cooking, for instance, it may happen that we must keep a roast in the oven, say, 25 minutes for each pound. If there are 4 1/2 pounds, that means 112 1/2 minutes, and it takes a little while to figure that that means 1 hour 52 1/2 minutes.

Suppose though, we were dealing with metric time units and that it was 25 "metric minutes" per pound of roast. Then 4 1/2 times 25 would be 112.5 "metric minutes," which would be 1.125 "metric hours" or, if you wish, 1 "metric hour" 12 "metric minutes" 50 "metric seconds." In handling all time measurements less than a day, conversion would only involve shifting decimal points, as you see.

I think it is a pity the committee didn't try to establish some such system. They might have succeeded if they had tied it in with the rest of the metric system, and it might have simplified at least one important part of time measurement.

DIMENSIONS

We now have all the basic units I will have room to talk about in this book. They fall into three groups: length, mass, and time. From these, more complicated units can be developed by taking the basic units in combination. Some complex units might involve both mass and length; or both length and time; or both mass and time; or all three.

In order to avoid getting lost among these combinations, I will introduce the notion of *dimensions*. When any quantity is measured in terms of units of mass, it is said to have the dimension M (for mass). If it is measured in terms of units of length, it has the dimension L (for length), and if in terms of units of time, it has the dimension T (for time).

Any two measures with identical dimensions can be manipulated arithmetically without trouble.

Any units of length, for instance, whether common, metric, or miscellaneous, can be added. You can find the sum of 2 versts, plus 5 miles, plus 3 kilometers, provided you know all the conversion figures involved. In the same way you can add 5 pounds and 1230 grams; or 4 hours and 105 minutes.

Of course, you cannot add two measurements of differing dimensions. You can't add 4 pounds to 5 inches; or 6 days to 17 kilograms. There are no conversion factors between measurements with different dimensions.

This may strike you as quite obvious. No one is very likely to try to add ounces and minutes, after all, or to subtract inches from gallons. However, once we start getting into some of the more complex units that I will discuss in the second half of this book, matters won't be quite that simple. In the case of complex units, it is sometimes necessary for engineers and scientists to work out the dimensions of each measurement carefully just to make sure they don't try to do the equivalent of adding inches and pounds without realizing it.

This careful checking of the dimensions of all measures is called *dimensional analysis*.

To deal most simply with dimensional analysis, it is best to take one particular unit in each of the three basic dimensions. If you do that, you can concentrate on the dimensions themselves and not be confused by sudden changes of units within the dimensions—say, from miles to kilometers or from gallons to liters. Of course, that raises the problem of which particular unit in each basic dimension ought to be chosen.

In the case of time, there was little argument. Everyone seems to have agreed on the second as the unit of choice.

In the case of mass and length, however, there are three sets of units in common use. Two sets are taken from the metric system. The unit of mass may be set equal to the gram and the unit of length to the centimeter. The alternative is to have the unit of mass the kilogram and the unit of length the meter. Both the gram-centimeter choice and the kilogram-meter have their advantages as we shall see.

A third system is used only in the English-speaking countries. There the unit of mass is the avoirdupois pound (which I will henceforth refer to simply as the "pound"), while the unit of length is the foot.

Now then, since I will be referring to these three alternative systems of units constantly, I will make use of certain abbreviations for convenience. Let's write "gram" as *gm* and "kilogram" as *kg*. We can abbreviate "second" as *sec,* "meter" as *m,* and "centimeter" as *cm*. Finally, we can abbreviate "foot" at *ft* and "pound" as *lb*.

All these abbreviations are self-explanatory, except the one for pound. The *lb* abbreviation is customary throughout the English-speaking countries and is a hangover from the days when Latin was the language of scholarship and people used scraps of Latin whenever they could. The Latin word for pound is *libra* (meaning "scale," actually, which is the instrument on which the pound weight is used). The *lb* abbreviation harks back to *libra*.

(It is for this same reason that the symbol for the British pound sterling, the unit of currency, resembles a capital *L*, thus: £.)

The three systems used in working with dimensions can, therefore, be listed (using abbreviations) as follows:

(1) The *gm-cm-sec* system
(2) The *kg-m-sec* system
(3) The *ft-lb-sec* system

In naming the system it doesn't really matter in which order you list the types of units. In the *gm-cm-sec* and *kg-m-sec* systems, it seems customary to list the mass unit first and the length unit second. In the *ft-lb-sec* system, the length unit comes first. I repeat, this is a matter of usage and habit and doesn't really matter.

SWITCHING SYSTEMS

In order to switch from one system to another (as I will have to do constantly from now on) we must have the conversion factors for the individual units involved. The unit of time, at least, gives us no trouble; it is *sec* in all three systems.

The two systems based on metric measurements give us very little more trouble in mass and length either. It is easy to remember that 1 *kg* = 1,000 *gm* and that 1 *gm* = 0.001 *kg*; or that 1 *m* = 100 *cm* and that 1 *cm* = 0.01 *m*. It is only the *ft-lb-sec* system that introduces real complications, because there the units of mass and length don't fit in evenly with the units used in the other systems.

For instance, in the units of length:

$$1 \ ft \ = 30.48 \quad cm = 0.3048 m$$
$$1 \ cm = \ \ 0.03281 \ ft$$
$$1 \ m \ = \ \ 3.281 \quad ft$$

(Notice that the conversion factors involved in the *ft-cm* changeover differ from those in the *ft-m* changeover only by a change in the position of the decimal point. This is thanks to the decimal nature of the metric system.)

Again, in the units of mass:

$$1 \ lb \ = 453.592 \quad gm$$
$$1 \ gm = \quad 0.002205 \quad lb$$
$$1 \ kg = \quad 2.205 \quad lb$$

Once we have these conversion figures, we can change any unit belonging to the *ft-lb-sec* system into one belonging to either the *gm-cm-sec* or *kg-m-sec* systems, and vice versa.

As an example, let's begin by considering units of area. To measure the area of a rectangle it is only necessary to measure the lengths of two adjoining sides and multiply those lengths. To measure the area of a triangle, half the length of one side is multiplied by the length of the altitude upon that side. In other types of figures, the details differ, but always it boils down to multiplying one length by another.

The dimensions of area, therefore, are length multiplied by length, or $L \times L$. It is customary in algebra to symbolize such a multiplication of a quantity by itself as L^2 (which is read "L square"). The exact unit by which this dimension can be expressed depends on the system of units being used. In the *gm-cm-sec* system, the unit of an area is $cm \times cm$, naturally.

Previously, in this book, I explained that when 1 foot was multiplied by 1 foot, the result was 1 square foot. Similarly, 1 centimeter multiplied by 1 centimeter yields 1 square centimeter. "Square centimeter" can be abbreviated "sq. cm." and often is. However, in the treatment of systems of units, it is customary to handle *cm* just as though it were an algebraic symbol. Just as $L \times L$ is L^2, so $cm \times cm$ is cm^2, which is read "centimeter squared" or "square centimeter" as you choose.

Similarly, the unit of area in the *ft-lb-sec* system is ft^2 (which may be read "foot squared" or "square foot"); and in the *kg-m-sec* system, it is m^2 ("meter *squared*" or "square meter").

The relationship between the standard units of area can be obtained from the relationship between the standard units of distance. Since 1 $ft = 30.48 \ cm$, then 1 $ft^2 = (30.48 \ cm)^2$. The numbers and the units can be squared separately so that: $1 \ ft^2 = (30.48)^2 \ cm^2$. By working out the squares of the numbers we end with:

$$1 \ ft^2 = 929.03 \ cm^2$$

By using the conversion factor changing cm to ft, or m to ft, in the same way, we find that:

$$1 \ cm^2 = 0.0010764 \ ft^2$$
$$1 \ m^2 = 10.764 \quad ft^2$$

When we get to the standard unit of volume, we need only go one step further. All volumes can be determined by multiplying a length by a length by a length. In the case of a parallelepiped (such as an ordinary box), this simply means the multiplication of the lengths of any three edges

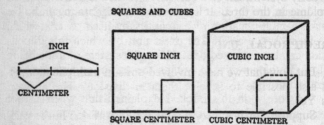

SQUARES AND CUBES

INCH

CENTIMETER

SQUARE INCH

SQUARE CENTIMETER

CUBIC INCH

CUBIC CENTIMETER

that meet at a point. In the case of other solids, the matter is more complicated but still boils down to length times length times length.

The dimensions of volume are therefore $L \times L \times L$, or L^3. In the various systems, the standard units for volume are cm^3 ("centimeter cubed" or "cubic centimeter"), ft^3 ("foot cubed" or "cubic foot"), and m^3 ("meter cubed" or "cubic meter").

Sometimes, "cubic centimeter" is abbreviated as cc by chemists, but this habit appears to be dwindling and I am glad of it. It is a confusing abbreviation, too easily confused with cm itself.

The relationship between the cubic units of volume are worked out just as those between the square units of area were. The only difference is that the conversion figures involved in the standard units of length are cubed instead of squared. For instance, since $1\ ft = 30.48\ cm$, $1\ ft^3 = (30.48)^3\ cm^3$. The results are:

$$1\ ft^3 = 28,317\ cm^3$$

and:

$$1\ cm^3 = 0.000035314\ ft^3$$
$$1\ m^3 = 35.314\ \qquad ft^3$$

(In all this, you must not confuse the standard unit with the most customary unit. The most customary unit of volume among scientists is the liter, or, for small volumes, the milliliter. Nevertheless, for purposes of dimensional analysis, and for the reduction of all types of units into an orderly system, cm^3, m^3, and ft^3 are the standard units of volume in the three unit systems I am discussing.)

RECIPROCAL UNITS

But now that we have involved units in multiplication, is it also possible to involve them in division? The answer is Yes.

Suppose, for instance, that you are interested in the rate at which a wheel is turning (a bicycle wheel, an automobile wheel, a gyroscope, or any wheel). Imagine you have a device which enables you to count the number of times the wheel turns while a stop watch is enabling you to measure the time during which it turns.

You may find, as a result, that the wheel makes 240 revolutions in 80 seconds. It is customary to express this as so many revolutions in one second. To determine this (assuming that the wheel is turning at a constant rate), you must divide the 240 revolutions by 80 seconds.

It is easy to divide 240 by 80; the answer is 3. But what happens to the units? You have to say:

$$\frac{240\ \text{revolutions}}{80\ \text{seconds}} = \frac{3\ \text{revolutions}}{1\ \text{second}} = 3\ \text{revolutions/second}$$

The final expression can be read as "3 revolutions per second." The word "per" means "for each" so that this is equivalent to saying "3 revolutions for each second."

Now "revolution" is not the type of unit that fits into the *MLT* scheme so it is more convenient to remove it. Instead of saying, "The wheel turns at the rate of 3 revolutions per second," we say: "The number of revolutions of the wheel is 3 per second."

Remembering that the word "per" was used to represent a fraction mark, we can symbolize "3 per second" as "3/*sec*."

In other words, the dimension of rate of rotation is /*T*. In all three systems, the standard unit would be /*sec*. This is usually read as "per second," but it may be referred to also as *reciprocal second*. In algebra, 1/*a* is the reciprocal of *a*; therefore, by analogy, 1/*sec* is the reciprocal of *sec* and is called that.

It is perfectly possible that you may be interested in the turning of a wheel, not with respect to time, but with respect to distance. That is, you may want to know how many times a bicycle wheel turns while you travel a certain distance, regardless of the time it takes to travel that distance. You would then divide the number of revolutions by the distance and come out with so many revolutions per unit distance.

The dimensions of revolutions per distance would be /*L*. Here, there would be different standard units, depending upon the system used. We can talk of the number of revolutions per centimeter, per foot, or per meter. The units would be, respectively, /*cm*, /*ft*, or /*m*.

It is possible to convert /*cm* into /*ft* as follows: Knowing that 1 *ft* = 30.48 *cm,* then 1/*ft* = 1/ (30.48 *cm*) = 1/30.48 × /*cm*. Or: 1/*ft* = 0.03281/*cm*.

If you will compare this with the relationship between *ft* and *cm,* you may detect what seems to be a coincidence. After all, 1 *cm* / 0.03281 *ft*. The conversion factors are the same. Coincidence, really?

No. It is a general rule that if two units of the same dimensions are changed into reciprocals, the conversion factor remains the same, but in reverse. For instance, if

e know that 1 yard equals 3 feet, then 1 revolution per
ot is equal to 3 revolutions per yard. That makes sense,
oesn't it? Well it amounts to saying that:

$$1 \text{ yard} = 3 \text{ feet}$$
$$1/\text{foot} = 3/\text{yard}$$

In the same way, if we know that $1 \, m = 3.28 \, ft$, we can
ll at once that $1/ft = 3.28/m$.

It is also possible to have reciprocal units of mass, with
imensions of $/M$. If you were interested in the number
f bacteria per mass of earth, or the number of cells per
ass of tissue, you could express that quantity either as
er gram ($/gm$), per pound ($/lb$), or per kilogram ($/kg$),
ccording to the system being used.

The relationship between the reciprocal units of mass
re simple enough. Since $1 \, lb = 453.592 \, gm$ and since 1
g = 2.205 \, lb$, it follows that:

$$1/gm = 453.592/lb$$
$$1/lb = 2.205/kg$$

Pounds per Cubic Foot and
Centimeters per Second

COMBINING THE UNITS

So far, all the types of measurements I have discussed have involved only one kind of unit. It has been either L, M, or T. Units such as $1/L$ (as the reciprocal centimeter, or L^3 (as the cubic centimeter) are units that still involve only L.

But what of measurements that may involve more than one type of unit? Consider the *density* of an object. That represents the mass of a particular volume of a substance and is a measure of considerable importance to chemists, physicists, and engineers.

Density varies from substance to substance. For instance, 1 milliliter of water has a mass of 1 gram; but a milliliter of mercury would have a mass of 13.596 grams. A milliliter of liquid hydrogen would have a mass of only 0.07 gram. (These figures vary with the temperature, somewhat. This is important to the scientist but in this book I am concentrating on the units, and matters such a variation with temperature I will reluctantly ignore.)

Density can be expressed as so much mass contained in so much volume. More concisely: density equals mass per volume. Since the dimensions of mass are M, and of volume are L^3, it follows that the dimensions of density are M/L^3.

This can be expressed in three different ways in the three systems: in the *gm-cm-sec* system, the units of density are gm/cm^3 ("grams per cubic centimeter"). In the *ft-lb-sec* system, it is lb/ft^3 ("pounds per cubic foot"). And in the *kg-m-sec* system, it is kg/m^3 ("kilograms per cubic meter"). The examples I gave two paragraphs above are in the *gm-cm-sec* system. The density of water is 1 *gm/cm³*, that of mercury is 13.596 *gm/cm³* and of liquid hydrogen 0.07 *gm/cm³*.

Now suppose you wanted to convert from one system of units to the other, say from *lb/ft³* to *gm/cm³*.

We already know that 1 *lb* = 453.592 *gm* and that 1 *ft* = 30.48 *cm*. Therefore: 1 *lb/ft³* = (453.592 gm)/(30.48 cm)³. If we separate the figures and the units, this becomes: 1 *lb/ft³* = 453.592/ (30.48) ³ *gm/cm³*. Only arithmetic is now needed to tell us that:

$$1 \ lb/ft^3 = 0.0160 \ gm/cm^3$$

Using the same principle, we can also show that:

$$1 \ gm/cm^3 = 62.43 \ lb/ft^3$$

Since the density of water is 1 *gm/cm³*, we can tell from the conversion factors given immediately above, that it must also be 62.43 *lb/ft³*.

Another way of saying this is that a cubic centimeter of water has a mass of 1 gram; that a cubic foot of water has a mass of 62.43 pounds.

Turning to the other substances I have mentioned, the density of mercury being 13.596 *gm/cm³*, it is also 13.596 × 62.43 or 848.80 *lb/ft³*. As for liquid hydrogen, its density being 0.07 *gm/cm³*, it is also 0.07 × 62.43 or 4.37 *lb/ft³*.

ELIMINATING THE UNITS

Although conversion from one system to another, as I have just shown you, involves only simple arithmetic and calls for no great strain on the mind, it is tedious. Sometimes, therefore, a device is used to make conversions unnecessary. The measurement of density, as it happens, involves one of the most familiar examples of this device, so here is my chance to explain it.

The fact that the density of water is 1 *gm/cm³* suggests that water might be used as a reference material in the measurement of density. Why not compare the density of all other substances to water? In other words, instead of saying that mercury has such and such a density, we could say that it is 13.596 times as dense as water; or that liquid hydrogen is 0.07 times as dense as water.

When we say this, we are expressing a *ratio;* that is, we are comparing one measurement with another of the same type. (It must be of the same type.) But how do we know how many times denser than water mercury or liquid hydrogen are? Why, we divide their densities by that of water. Thus:

$$\frac{\text{density of mercury}}{\text{density of water}} = \frac{13.596 \ gm/cm^3}{1 \ gm/cm^3} = 13.596$$

The important thing about this division is that gm/cm^3 is present above and below the fraction line and cancels out, just as in the algebraic expression $2a/3a$, the a would cancel out leaving $2/3$.

The result is that the ratio, 13.596, has no units. It is a *dimensionless quantity;* or as it is sometimes called, a *pure number*. This ratio of densities is called *specific gravity*. (The specific gravity also varies with the temperature —of both the mercury and the water—but we won't worry about that. It is only a slight variation, anyway.)

You can even get the specific gravity of water by comparing its density to itself: $1 \ gm/cm^3 \div 1 \ gm/cm^3$ yields the quotient 1 and so the specific gravity of water is 1.

Do you see the difference between density and specific gravity now? The densities of mercury, water, and liquid hydrogen are, respectively, $13.596 \ gm/cm^3$, $1 \ gm/cm^3$ and $0.07 \ gm/cm^3$. The specific gravities of the same substances are, respectively, 13.596, 1, and 0.07.

You may not think this is enough of a difference to make a fuss about. After all, what's the difference you say that the density is $13.596 \ gm/cm^3$ or that the specific gravity is 13.596. The number is the same in both cases. Is there so much of an advantage in just saving breath by leaving out the units?

There's more to it than that. Suppose you consider the

density of mercury in lb/ft^3, as given earlier in this chapter, and compare that with the density of water in lb/ft^3.

$$\frac{\text{density of mercury}}{\text{density of water}} = \frac{848.80 \quad lb/ft^3}{62.43 \quad lb/ft^3} = 13.596$$

The ratio of the densities (*i.e.,* the specific gravity) is the same regardless of the system of units being used! In other words, the specific gravity of mercury is 13.596 in the *gm-cm-sec* system, in the *ft-lb-sec* system, in the *kg-m-sec* system, or in any other system you care to make up.

This is true of all dimensionless quantities. Whenever you can use a dimensionless quantity, you not only save breath, you also save all concern about dimensions and conversions from one system to another.

There is another well-known example of this in a measurement that would ordinarily have the units of mass. The individual atoms have masses that have now been determined quite accurately by scientists. Naturally, these masses are extremely small by everyday standards. The most common variety of hydrogen atom (the least massive known) has a mass of 0.000000000000000000000016617 *gm.* The most common variety of oxygen atom is almost sixteen times more massive but is still only 0.00000000000000000000000026372 gm.

One way of getting around the use of such small numbers is to compare the masses of the various atoms and use the ratios instead of the numbers themselves. (At the time it first became customary to do this, there was another advantage. Chemists did not know the actual masses with great accuracy but could nevertheless determine the ratios accurately.)

Since the hydrogen atom has the smallest mass, it would be the natural one to use for comparison. Another type of atom could be said to be "so many times more massive than the hydrogen atom." Actually, this was done for a while, but then chemists decided to use the oxygen atom as the basis for comparison. There were good chemical reasons for this. Comparison with oxygen made for less difficult chemical manipulations than comparison with any other atom.

If oxygen atoms were used as basis for comparison, however, any atom with a mass less than that of an oxygen atom (the hydrogen atom, for instance) would yield a figure less than one. To avoid this, chemists decided to multiply the ratio by 16. In that way, the number obtained for even the hydrogen atom would be over one. The ratio multiplied by 16 is called the *mass number* and the mass number of the most common hydrogen atom would therefore be:

$$\frac{0.00000000000000000000000016617}{0.00000000000000000000000026372} \times 16 = 1.00816$$

The mass number of the oxygen atom itself comes out to 16.0000 since you have the ratio of the mass of the oxygen atom to itself, which is 1, and multiply that by 16.

(Most of the elements, as they occur in nature, are made up of similar, but not identical, atoms. The different varieties, called *isotopes,* have different mass numbers. For instance, there is an isotope of hydrogen with a mass number of 2.01474, about double that of the ordinary hydrogen atom. The average mass of these isotopes in the proportions in which they naturally occur is called the *atomic weight*. Chemists had calculated the atomic weight long before they knew that isotopes existed, and the term "atomic weight" is still much more common than "mass number." Further, they did not use the most common oxygen atom as the basis of comparison, but the mixture of three different oxygen isotopes. For that reason there are old-fashioned "chemical atomic weights" and newfashioned "physical atomic weights." Again, these are complications we need not concern ourselves with.)

In any case, the mass number offers us a device for expressing the mass of an atom in a dimensionless fashion. The mass numbers of the two naturally occurring uranium isotopes are 238.1252 and 235.1175 (which is why we speak of uranium-238 and uranium-235). It is not necessary to ask 238.1252 what? 235.1175 what? It isn't 238.-

1252 grams or inches or anything else, just 238.1252. And of course these mass numbers are the same whatever unit system we care to use.

I must repeat a precaution I have already given in a hasty aside. In setting up a ratio, it is necessary to have both measurements in identical units if you expect the units to cancel. You cannot take a ratio of the density of mercury in gm/cm^3 and that of water in lb/ft^3. That would be 13.59 gm/cm^3/62.43 lb/ft^3. Undoubtedly you could divide 13.59 by 62.43, but what would you do with the units? They would not cancel out and you would not have a dimensionless quantity.

THE SPEED OF LIGHT

Another very common measurement involving two different types of units is *speed*. Speed is the rate of change of position with time. That is, you may be here now and a mile away at some later time, thus changing position with time. The faster you do so, the greater your speed. If you move from here to a mile away in ten minutes, you have been moving with greater speed than if you completed the same motion in twenty minutes.

Consequently, to find your speed (or, at any rate, your average speed) you must divide the total distance traveled by the total time elapsed during the traveling. To travel 20 miles in 2 hours is to travel 20 miles/2 hours or 10 miles/hour. Similarly, to travel 30 miles in 3 hours is also to travel 10 miles/hour, whereas to travel 15 miles in half an hour is to travel 15 miles 1/2 hour or 30 miles/hour.

The dimension of speed, then, is length divided by time, of L/T. To express speed in standard units by each of our three systems, we must use *cm/sec*, *ft/sec*, or *m/sec*.

Since 1 *ft* equals 30.48 *cm;* then 1 *ft/sec* = (30.48 *cm*) /*sec*, or:

$$1 \; ft/sec = 30.48 \; cm/sec$$

As you see, the fact that the "per second" is the same on both sides means that the conversion factor doesn't change.

You can say that 1 *ft/sec* is as much greater than 1 *cm/sec*, as 1 *ft* is greater than 1 *cm*.

Using this general rule, and knowing that 1 *m* = 3.281 *ft*, we can say at once, that:

$$1 \ m/sec = 3.281 \ ft/sec$$

And so for other similar conversions as well.

However, "per second" is not commonly used in everyday life in connection with speeds. Usually we express the speed of automobiles or airplanes in miles per hour. People outside the English-speaking nations express it as kilometers per hour. How do such units fit in with the standard units?

Well, 1 mile = 5280 feet and 1 hour = 3600 seconds. Consequently, 1 mile/hour = (5280 *ft*)/(3600 *sec*) = 5280/3600 *ft/sec*. Thus:

$$1 \ \text{mile/hour} = 1.4611 \ ft/sec$$

And so if you are traveling in a car going 60 miles an hour, you are traveling at the rate of 60 × 1.4611, or about 88 *ft/sec*. If you are in an airplane flying at the speed of 300 miles/hour, you are traveling at the rate of 300 × 1.4611 or about 438 *ft/sec*.

If we switch to kilometers per hour and remember that 1 kilometer equals 100,000 *cm* while an hour is equal to 3600 *sec*, we find that 1 kilometer/hour = (100,000 *cm*)/(3600 *sec*) × 100,000/3600 *cm/sec*, or:

$$1 \ \text{kilometer/hour} = 27.78 \ cm/sec$$

The most famous speed in science is the speed of light in a vacuum. That is usually expressed (in English-speaking countries, at least) as miles/*sec*. The best measurements currently available give the speed of light as 186,272 miles/*sec*.

In countries using the metric system, the speed of light is usually given as kilometers/*sec*. Since 1 mile = 1.60934 kilometers, 1 mile/*sec* equals 1.60934 kilometers/*sec*. (Re-

THE SPEED OF LIGHT

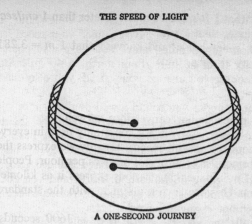

A ONE-SECOND JOURNEY

member, adding a "per second" on each side doesn't change the conversion factor.) Consequently, the speed of light is $186,272 \times 1.60934$, or $299,778$ kilometers/*sec*.

VELOCITY

In ordinary speech, the word *velocity* (from a Latin word meaning "swift") is treated as though it were synonymous with the Anglo-Saxon-derived "speed."

To scientists, there is a difference in the words that goes beyond the language of derivation. Speed is merely the rate of change of position with time. Velocity is the rate of change of position with time, in a specific direction.

For instance, if you are traveling at 60 miles/hour in an automobile headed due north, your speed is 60 miles/hour. Your velocity, however, is 60 miles/hour north. The "north" is essential if you are expressing velocity.

If, as you are traveling, someone else passes you on the other side of the highway, going 60 miles an hour to the south, you are both traveling at the same speed. You are both going 60 miles/hour. You are not, however, both traveling at the same velocity. You are going 60 miles/hour north. He is going 60 miles/hour south.

Now suppose you slow down your rate of travel to

the point where you are going only 40 miles/hour, but are still heading north. You have changed your speed from 60 miles/hour to 40 miles/hour. You have also changed your velocity from 60 miles/hour north to 40 miles/hour north. Whenever you change your speed, you also change your velocity.

However, suppose you round a well-banked curve without slackening your speed or changing it in the slightest and, in the end, are traveling due east. You have not changed speed. You have maintained a steady 60 miles/hour while taking the curve. But you have changed velocity. You began by going 60 miles/hour north and you ended going 60 miles/hour east. It is possible, therefore, to change velocity without changing speed.

Better still, consider the earth. It travels about the sun in a path that is very close to a circle. For our purposes, let's pretend it is a circle. It travels at an average speed of about 18.5 miles per second as compared to the sun. (In standard units, this is equal to 29,800 *m/sec,* or to 97,700 *ft/sec,* or to 2,980,000 *cm/sec.*) This rate of travel is not quite constant, but it would be if the earth's orbit were a perfect circle, as we are assuming.

We can say then that the earth travels about the sun at a constant speed, which is always 18.5 miles/*sec.* However, it is not traveling at a constant velocity. In fact, it doesn't even have a velocity in the ordinary meaning of the word, since its velocity is changing every instant. As it travels in a circle, you see, it is moving in a different direction, and therefore has a different velocity every instant of time.

I have introduced the notion of velocity now because it will be important in the next chapter, where I will discuss changes in speed and in direction of motion. I will use the term "velocity" from now on, instead of "speed," in order to cover both types of change.

Dynes and Newtons

ETERNAL MOTION

Let's suppose we are dealing with a velocity that is changing. A common example is that of an automobile which is starting up. To begin with, it is not moving at all. One second after it has started it is moving, let us say, at the rate of 1 *ft/sec*. After another second, it is moving at 2 *ft/sec*. After still another second it is moving at 3 *ft/sec*. and so on.

Each second, its velocity increases by 1 *ft/sec*. A changing velocity is called an *acceleration* (from a Latin word meaning "hastening"). We can say that, in the example I have given, the acceleration is 1 *ft/sec* per second.

Since we always allow "per" to be represented by a fraction line, we can say that the acceleration is 1 *(ft/sec)/sec,* which can be read as "foot per second per second."

This expression can be simplified further, if we treat the units as though they were ordinary algebraic symbols. For instance: $(1/a)/a$ is equal to $1/a \div a$ or $1/a \times 1/a$ or $1/a^2$. By analogy, $(ft/sec)sec$ can be written ft/sec^2, which is read "foot per second squared."

The dimensions of acceleration, therefore, are L/T^2. In the *ft-lb-sec* system, this is ft/sec^2, as mentioned just above. In the two metric systems of units, it is m/sec^2 and cm/sec^2.

Because all three of these units have a "per second squared" in them, the conversion factor among them is the same as that involved in the length unit alone. Thus, to convert ft/sec^2 to cm/sec^2 the same factor is used as to convert *ft* to *cm*. Since 1 *ft* = 30.48 *cm,* 1 ft/sec^2 = 30.48 cm/sec^2, and so for other conversions as well.

But what causes an acceleration? It wasn't until the time of Isaac Newton in 1683 that science received an acceptable

99

explanation. Newton then presented his Laws of Motion
These were rules intended to explain the manner in which
objects moved, and they have proven satisfactory eve
since. There are three Laws, but I will consider only the
first two.

Newton's first law states that the velocity of any body
will not change if it is left completely to itself. (Notice
that I use the word "velocity.") This means that an objec
that is moving will continue to move, if left to itself, at the
same speed and in the same direction forever. The velocity
may be zero, of course, so the law also states that an objec
at rest will remain at rest forever, if left to itself.

His second law states that when the velocity of a body
does change, it is the result of something called a force
acting upon it. The greater the velocity-change, or acceleration, the greater the force.

Thus, when a car starts and begins to go faster and faster
it is because of the force being applied to it by the engine
If a golf ball curves in its flight (remember that curving is
an example of acceleration because it represents change
of direction, hence changing velocity, even if the speed of
the ball doesn't vary), it is because of the force of air pres
sure upon it as it spins.

This was a revolutionary viewpoint. Before Newton
scientists had observed that all motions on earth seemed
to come to a halt all by themselves. If you kick a piece of
wood, it will slide along the ground, then come to a halt
If you strike a hockey puck and send it skimming along
ice, it will move farther, but eventually it will come to a
halt even if it is left completely alone and strikes nothing

Scientists assumed, therefore, that a force was needed
to keep objects moving. Newton said No, the force was
needed to make them stop. An object skittering along the
ground is stopped by frictional forces. Even a hockey puck
on ice meets slight friction from the ice and the force of
air resistance as well. If there were no air and the ice were
perfectly frictionless, the puck would move forever.

Newton's laws explained the reason why the planets
moved eternally through the sky. Earlier astronomers had
thought that the laws governing motion in the heavens were

different from those governing motion on the earth. Or else they thought a constant force was being applied to the planets; perhaps gods or angels were pushing them. Newton pointed out that there was simply nothing to stop them, so they moved forever. (A very daring and simple notion which seemed completely against common sense. Often new ideas in science seem against common sense, until we get used to them.)

Of course, the planets do undergo acceleration. They travel around the sun in a curving path so that their velocity changes from instant to instant, even though their speed changes only slightly. The moon, similarly, travels about the earth. In order to explain this, Newton had to invent forces working on the moon and the planets to account for the acceleration. He therefore worked out his Law of Universal Gravitation in which every body in the universe exerted an attractive force on every other body.

(Now you see why scientists prefer to use the notion of "velocity" rather than of "speed." A force such as gravitation may alter a body's speed without altering its direction, as the case of a falling rock. Or it may alter a body's direction without altering its speed very much, as in the case of the earth circling about the sun. Should scientists then assume there are two kinds of gravity? If an object traveled about the sun in a long ellipse, as a comet does, it would change its speed considerably as well as its direction. Should a scientist suppose two kinds of gravity were working on it simultaneously? No, by using the concept of "velocity" to combine both speed and direction, he needs deal with only one type of force and he is much happier for the simplificaton.)

Now the strength of a force is measured not only by the acceleration it brings about, but also by the mass of the object. As long as you confine yourself to one body, force and acceleration match exactly. If you increase the force, you increase the acceleration by an equal amount.

Suppose, though, that you exert the same force on two different bodies. A massive body is accelerated only slightly; a light one is accelerated greatly. You may test this yourself. Kick a beach ball with all your might and you

will see it accelerate from rest to a speedy flight in a second
or so. If you were to kick a cannon ball with all your
might, however, you would set up a mere trickle of motion
(and possibly break your toe besides).

To measure a force, then, you need to know the mass
of an object and the acceleration imposed upon it. Scientists express this by saying "force = mass × acceleration."

SAVING SYLLABLES

The dimensions of mass are M, of course, and the
dimensions of acceleration, as I explained at the beginning
of the chapter, are L/T^2. If we are to multiply mass and
acceleration in order to measure force, we must multiply
the dimensions, too. The expression $M × L/T^2$ can be
written, according to the rules of algebra, as ML/T^2 and
that is the dimension of force.

In the three systems of units I have been discussing,
force may be expressed as $gm\ cm/sec^2$, $ft\ lb/sec^2$, and kg
m/sec^2. These are read: "gram-centimeter per second
squared," "foot-pound per second squared," and "kilogram-
meter per second squared." Notice that in the first and
third of these expressions I place the unit of mass first,
while in the second I place the unit of length first. This is
mere custom. It doesn't matter whether you say "foot
pound" or "pound-foot." It is just that most people are
in the habit of saying "foot-pound" (which is LM), even
though they are also in the habit of saying "gram-centimeter" (which is ML). There is no arguing with habit.

To show how the units work, suppose that a certain
force applied to an object that is 10 gm in mass causes an
acceleration of 5 cm/sec^2. The size of the force is therefore 10 gm × 5 cm/sec^2, or 50 $gm\ cm/sec^2$.

To convert units of force from one system to another
follows the principles already used.

$$1\ kg\ m/sec^2 = 100,000\ gm\ cm/sec^2$$
$$1\ kg\ m/sec^2 = 7.074\ ft\ lb/sec^2$$
$$1\ ft\ lb/sec^2 = 13,825.4\ gm\ cm/sec^2$$

You will probably not be very surprised if I tell you that as units grow more complicated, it becomes wearisome to write them every time, or to say them if you happen to be talking. Scientists are as lazy as anyone and it was a natural impulse to invent a kind of code monosyllable that would represent the phrase "gramcentimeter per secon squared" which they were always having to use. In place of its nine syllables, they invented a single syllable, *dyne,* from a Greek word meaning "strength" or "force."

Whenever a physicist says "1 dyne" he means "1 gramcentimeter per second squared." The two are merely different ways of saying the same thing, the first being a breath- and effort-saver. To put it down in black and white:

$$1 \text{ dyne} = 1 \ gm \ cm/sec^2$$

In calculating a force, then (to use the example given at the beginning of this section), we may multiply 10 *gm* by 5 *cm/sec²* and come out with 50 dynes.

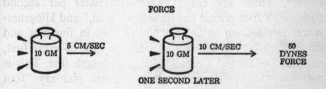

FORCE

10 GM — 5 CM/SEC

10 GM — 10 CM/SEC — 50 DYNES FORCE

ONE SECOND LATER

(Scientists are not the only ones who short-cut units. The speed of ships is usually expressed as "nautical miles per hour." Sailors replace these six syllables by the monosyllable, *knot.* This derives from the fact that an early way of measuring ships' speeds involved trailing a knotted rope behind the ship. Thus, a ship which is moving at 15 knots is moving at 15 nautical miles per hour. Landsmen usually aren't used to short-cutting the "per hour" out of units of speed and they are uncomfortable with a simple 15 knots as a measure of speed. When they try to sound nautical, they generally say that a ship is traveling "15 knots per hour" and this must drive sailors to distraction.)

Now what about the *kg-m-sec* system, which has its

units of force expressed as *kg m/sec²*. This, too, requires a short-cut code word. Instead of "kilogram-meter per second squared" (nine syllables), scientists say "newton" (two syllables). Physicists might as easily have invented a monosyllable for the purpose, but since Isaac Newton invented our modern notions of force, it seemed only right to honor him by applying his name to a unit of force. Therefore:

$$1 \text{ newton} = 1 \ kg \ m/sec^2$$

Of course, since I have already pointed out that 1 *kg m/sec²* equals 100,000 *gm cm/sec²*, we can also say that:

$$1 \text{ newton} = 100,000 \text{ dynes}$$

This shows the convenience of having two systems of units using the metric system. We end up with two units of force that are widely separated. The *gm-cm-sec* system puts forces in dynes and this is a convenient unit for small forces. The *kg-m-sec* system puts forces in newtons and this is a convenient unit for larger forces.

The *ft-lb-sec* system also has a special name for its unit of force, the *ft lb/sec²*. It is *poundal*. In other words:

$$1 \text{ poundal} = 1 \ ft \ lb/sec^2$$

From the relationship among the units of force already worked out in this section, we can say:

$$1 \text{ newton} = 7.074 \text{ poundals}$$
$$1 \text{ poundal} = 13,825.4 \text{ dynes}$$

THE CONFUSION OF WEIGHT

The commonest and best-known force—one to which we are all subjected—is that of *gravity*. It is gravitational force that holds the moon in its orbit about the earth and forces it to accelerate constantly as it moves in its curved path. (A change in direction is one form of an acceleration, I repeat again.) It also holds the earth in its orbit about the sun; and it holds the sun and the other stars in the galaxy rotating about a common galactic center.

What is easier to observe is that gravity also causes objects to accelerate downward (*i.e.*, fall at a faster and faster rate) if they are released about the surface of the earth.

The amount of gravitational force upon a falling object depends on several things. For one thing it depends on the mass of the falling object. If the mass of the falling object is doubled, the force of gravity is also doubled. But force equals mass times acceleration. This can be expressed briefly as $F = M \times A$. Elementary algebra tells us that this is the same as saying that $F/M = A$.

Now if mass is doubled and force is consequently also doubled, we have $2M/2 F$, which works out to M/F; since the 2's cancel. If we multiply mass by 15.4 (or any number) and find that the force also increases by 15.4 (or whatever the number is), then we have 15.4 $M/15.4 F$, which boils down to M/F still, and in every case, the M/F is equal to A the original A.

So you see, gravitational forces on the surface of the earth produce the same acceleration in all objects of whatever mass. This is just a fancy way of saying that all objects fall with the same velocity. It was the Italian scientist Galileo Galilei who first showed this by experiment about 1600. It was on Galileo's experiments, in fact, that Newton later based his three Laws of Motion, which are behind the algebraic explanation I have just given.

(It was difficult for scientists to understand this before Galileo's time, because the rule is only strictly true in a vacuum. Under actual conditions, air resistance slows the speed of fall. The less massive an object is and the more surface it presents to the air, the greater the effect of air resistance. Consequently, feathers, leaves, small pieces of paper, snowflakes, all fall very slowly when compared with blocks of wood, lumps of iron, and human beings. For many centuries, therefore, people wrongly believed that the heavier an object was, the faster it fell. It took the genius of Galileo to see past the obscuring effect of air resistance.)

Careful measurements have shown that a falling object will accelerate at a rate of about 980.6 *cm/sec*². Since a 1 *gm* mass will be accelerated in this fashion, the force of gravity is equal to 980.6 *gm cm/sec*². From this and from the conversion factors given in the previous section, we can see that the force of gravity equals 980.6 dynes, or 0.07093 poundal or 0.009806 newton.

(The acceleration of gravity, 980.6 *cm/sec*², is sometimes set equal to 1 *gal,* in honor of Galileo. A thousandth of this quantity, 0.9806 *cm/sec*², is therefore 1 *milligal.*)

Any discussion of gravity brings us back to mass. A massive object is pulled more strongly toward the earth by gravity than a light one is(though the acceleration is the same, as I have explained). This means that a more massive object presses down more heavily upon one's hand than a less massive one. This downward force is what we call *weight*.

Most people in ordinary life speak of the weight of an object when they really mean its mass. They talk of heavy objects instead of massive ones and so on. They can hardly be blamed. The notion of weight came first. It was only in the time of Galileo and, especially, of Newton that a clear notion of mass was introduced.

The physicist must make a clear distinction. Mass represents the amount of matter contained in a body and its units are grams, pounds, kilograms, and so on. Weight represents the force with which the body is attracted to the earth (or some other astronomical body, sometimes) and its units are (or should be) dynes, poundals, newtons, and so on.

However, the confusion between weight and mass seems permanent. A one-pound mass is said to have a weight of "one pound," a one-gram mass to have a weight of "one gram" and so on. There's not much that can be done about it. In this book, as I said at the beginning of Chapter 5, I have deliberately talked only of mass. It will be necessary, though, to talk of weight occasionally and, to prevent confusion, I will call a weight of one gram "1 gram(w)" and a weight of one pound "1 pound(w)" and so on. To make the distinction even sharper, I will not abbreviate gram, pound, and so on when I am talking of weight.

I will have to ask you to remember that 1 gram(w) represents a force and not a mass. I realize that this is difficult to do, the habits of everyday life being so strong.

Let's see what kind of a force 1 gram(w) is. The force of 1 gram(w) is obtained when we multiply a mass of 1 *gm* by the acceleration of gravity, which is 980.6 *cm/sec²*. The product of the two is 980.6 *gm cm/sec²* or 980.6 dynes. Consequently:

$$1 \text{ gram(w)} = 980.6 \quad \text{dynes}$$
$$1 \text{ dyne} = 0.001020 \text{ gram(w)}$$

Since 0.001020 gram(w) is equal to 1.020 milligrams (w), this is like saying that if you were to place a milligram mass on your hand, it would press downward with a force of just about 1 dyne. Try this, if you ever get a chemist friend to lend you the milligram "weight" he may use on his balance, and you will find the pressure against your hand so feathery that you will realize what a small unit of force a dyne is.

If we switch the acceleration of gravity to the *kg-m-sec* system, we find that 980.6 *cm/sec²* = 9.806 *m/sec²*. To find the force exerted by 1 kilogram(w) we must multiply this acceleration by 1 *kg* (since force equals mass times acceleration) and end with 9.806 *kg m/sec²*. Therefore:

$$1 \text{ kilogram(w)} = 9.806 \quad \text{newtons}$$
$$1 \text{ newton} = 0.1020 \text{ kilogram(w)}$$

Next, let's convert gravitational acceleration into the *ft-lb-sec* system. Since 1 *m* = 3.28 feet (or 3.2808 feet, to be more exact, in this particular case), the gravitational acceleration of 9.806 *m/sec²* can be expressed as (9.806 ×3.2808) or 32.17 *ft/sec²*. To get the force exerted by a mass of 1 *lb,* we must multiply that acceleration by the pound, and the force thus becomes 32.17 *ft lb/sec²*. And so:

$$1 \text{ pound(w)} = 32.17 \quad \text{poundals}$$
$$1 \text{ poundal} = 0.0311 \text{ pound(w)}$$

THE WEIGHTLESS CANNON BALL

You may wonder why I go to such pains to differentiate between mass and weight. If the two are inseparable, why not use the same units for both, and never mind that weight is a force and not a mass?

Ah, but mass and weight are not inseparable!

The force of gravitational attraction depends not only on the mass of the body being attracted, but also upon its distance from the center of the earth. If the earth were a perfect sphere, the distance between the center of the earth and the center of the body would always be the same. However, the earth is not a perfect sphere. It is slightly flattened at the poles.

At the poles a body is nearer the center of the earth than it would be at any other point on the earth's surface, and it is consequently attracted more strongly than anywhere else. As the body is moved farther and farther from the pole, it is attracted less and less strongly, until at the equator (at the height of the so-called equatorial "bulge") it is attracted least.

One of the reasons I gave the acceleration of gravity as being "about 980.6 cm/sec^2" is that it varies from place to place on the earth's surface. It is 980.6 at sea level just halfway between the equator and the poles, but at the

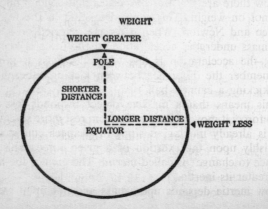

equator it is 978 *cm/sec²* *while at the poles it is* 983 *cm/sec²*.

Weight varies in proportion, since weight depends upon the force of gravity which, in turn, is measured by the amount of acceleration it gives rise to. Mass, however, does not vary. Mass is the amount of matter contained in an object and that is the same on the equator as at the poles or anywhere in between.

If one travels to a mountaintop, one is farther from the center of the earth. The force of gravity decreases there, and so does weight. Mass, however, is the same at the mountaintop as in the valley.

The force of gravity depends also upon the mass of the body that does the attracting—in our case, the earth. The mass of the earth does not vary, but suppose you were on the moon. The moon is a smaller body than the earth and its force of gravitational attraction is weaker. On the moon's surface, the force of gravity is only one-sixth that on the earth's surface. Weight is correspondingly decreased, but not mass. A mass of 1*lb* on the moon would weigh only 0.16 pound(w) but would still have a mass of 1 *lb*.

When an object is moving freely in response to gravitational forces (as when a satellite or a space station is in an orbit about the earth) there is no sensation of attraction to the earth. You would be weightless, but you would still have all your mass.

Now there are physical properties that depend on mass and not on weight. This showed up first in the work of Galileo and Newton. When a force is exerted on a mass that mass undergoes acceleration. If the force is kept the same, the acceleration is less when the mass is greater. (Remember the difference between kicking a beach ball and kicking a cannon ball.)

This means that a massive object responds less to a given force; it moves into motion from rest more sluggishly. If it is already moving, it stops or changes course more sluggishly upon the exertion of a given force. This "resistance to change" is called *inertia*. The greater the mass, the greater its inertia.

Now inertia depends upon mass and not upon weight.

If you were on a space station circling the earth, you would feel weightless, as I said, and so would everything else. If a large cannon ball were placed on your hand, you could support it with your little finger and feel no discomfort. It would weigh less than the beach ball on earth.

But suppose you put that feathery cannon ball at your feet and kicked it. Would it go sailing off into space like the super-light beach ball it seems to be? It would not! It would still have all its mass, and its inertia would depend upon that mass and not upon weight. That weightless cannon ball would still move forward only sluggishly as you kicked it, and you would still very likely break your toe.

On the surface of the earth, in other words, the average man can afford to confuse mass and weight. In everyday life, the confusion would cause no trouble. But we are on the threshold of the Age of Space, and on other worlds or in outer space a confusion of mass and weight might mean a question of life or death.

As for scientists, they can't afford to confuse the two even on the surface of the earth.

THE WEIGHT OF AIR

Sometimes force is applied over an area. For instance, the air all about us is pulled down by gravitational force. The weight of the air (that is, the force it exerts in all directions) is spread over the earth's surface. It is measured as so much force per unit area.

Now the dimensions of force, as I explained earlier in the chapter, are ML/T^2. The dimensions of area, as I explained in Chapter 6, are L^2. Consequently, to express force per area, we must divide ML/T^2 by L^2. Well, $ML/T^2 \div L^2 = ML/T^2 \times 1/L^2 = ML/T^2L^2 = M/LT^2$.

Force per area is called *pressure*. In the three systems of units I have been discussing, the units of pressure would be $gm/cm\ sec^2$, $lb/ft\ sec^2$, and $kg/m\ sec^2$.

Scientists, however, do not express the units of pressure in this way, generally speaking. They are more likely to express pressure as force per area directly. Thus, in the *gm-cm-sec* system, pressure could be expressed as dynes /cm². If we remember that a dyne is equal to a *gm cm/sec²*, then 1 dyne/cm² = 1 *gm cm/sec²/cm²*, and this works out to 1 *gm/cm sec²*. The two ways of expressing the unit of pressure are therefore equivalent:

$$1 \text{ dyne}/cm^2 = 1 \text{ } gm/cm \text{ } sec^2$$

In the other systems, the unit of pressure, on the same basis of force per area, would be poundals/*ft²* and newtons/*m²*.

Actually, though, the units of force that are most commonly used in expressing pressure are not the dyne, poundal, or newton, but the various weight units. For instance, the pressure of the atmosphere upon the surface of the earth has been measured and found to average (at sea level) 14.7 pounds(w) per square inch.

(It may seem strange to you that time is involved in pressure. Suppose you look at it this way, though. Pressure is the result of the collision of the molecules of matter with some surface. They collide, push and rebound, with the push representing the pressure. But at any instantaneous moment of time, some molecules have not yet struck, some have already struck and left, and some are in contact, but are not pushing. It is only with the passage of time that molecules have a chance to collide, push, and rebound, and that is why time is involved in pressure.)

Scientists work so frequently with a pressure equal to that of the air that they usually set the average air pressure equal to 1 *standard atmosphere,* called more simply 1 *atmosphere*. It follows that 1 atmosphere is equal to any of the values given just above.

For convenience, 1,000,000 dynes/*cm²* has been set equal to 1 *bar* (from a Greek word meaning "heavy"). The atmosphere and the bar are almost equal. Since 1 atmosphere equals 1,013,000 dynes/*cm²*, 1 atmosphere equals 1.013 bars.

A *millibar* (one thousandth of a bar) is equal to 1000 dynes/*cm²* and a *microbar* (one millionth of a bar), which is also called a *barye,* is equal to 1 dyne/*cm²*. The barye is therefore the standard unit of pressure in the *gm-cm-sec* system of units.

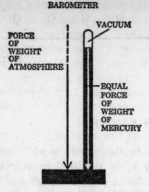

BAROMETER

VACUUM

FORCE
OF
WEIGHT
OF
ATMOSPHERE

EQUAL
FORCE
OF
WEIGHT
OF
MERCURY

The pressure of the atmosphere actually varies from time to time in any given place on the earth (by only a couple of per cent, however) and it varies with height above sea level. A mountaintop has lower air pressure than a valley.

The actual air pressure is measured by a *barometer,* which balances the weight of a column of mercury against the weight of the atmosphere. On the average, it takes a column of mercury 30 inches high to do this. The air pressure is presented by weather forecasters as so many "inches of mercury."

In terms of "inches of mercury":

1 atmosphere	= 30	inches of mercury
1 bar	= 29.6	inches of mercury
1 millibar	= 0.0296	inch of mercury
1 barye	= 0.0000296	inch of mercury

Here again is an example of how small a unit the dyne is. A film of mercury 1/30,000 of an inch thick presses down on a square centimeter of surface with a total pressure of one dyne.

Ergs and Watts

WORK MINUS EMOTION

Now we come to the word "work," which has an ugly sound to many of us because, in everyday life, work is something that takes a lot of effort and is done more or less involuntarily. The effort alone doesn't make something work, because there are few jobs of work that take as much effort, for instance, as a quick game of tennis. Yet, because tennis is something you do voluntarily for recreation, it is "fun" and not "work."

Again, when I am writing a book, my wife thinks I'm working (that's what I tell her), I think I'm having fun, and the neighbors think I'm loafing.

Physicists, however, use the word "work" in such a way as to eliminate any emotional feelings in the matter. To them, *work* is something that is accomplished when a force operates over a distance.

Thus, you do work when you exert force to lift an object against the force of gravity. If you lift that object 2 feet, you have done twice as much work as you would have done if you had lifted it 1 foot. Again, if you exert enough force to lift a 2-pound mass 1 foot against gravity, you have done twice as much work as you would have if you had exerted enough force to lift a 1-pound mass 1 foot against gravity.

Work is measured, then, by the force exerted multiplied by the distance through which it is exerted. To say this in shorthand fashion: work = force × distance.

As usual, units have to be considered. The dimensions of force are, as I have explained in the previous chapter, ML/T^2. The dimensions of distance are of course, L. Multiply these together and the dimensions of work turn out to be $ML/T^2 \times L$, or ML^2/T^2.

Using the standard units of our three systems, work may be expressed either as $gm\ cm^2/sec^2$, $lb\ ft^2/sec^2$, or $kg\ m^2/sec^2$. As an alternative, the units can be expressed just by combining the shorthand name for the unit of force and the unit of distance. That is, you can express the unit of work as dyne-*cm,* or poundal-*ft,* or newton-*m.*

But before I go any further, I wish to introduce the word *energy.* Energy can be defined as that property of a body which enables it to do work. (In fact, the word "energy" comes from Greek words meaning "work within." There is "work within" bodies containing energy.)

The property enabling a body to do work may involve the structure of the molecules making it up, or an electric current passing through it, a magnetic field permeating it, the heat that it contains, the motion it possesses, and a number of other things. These are all varieties of energy because they can all lead to the performance of work. During the nineteenth century, physicists found that the various forms of energy could be converted one into the other and that any of them could be converted to work. Furthermore, work could be converted into the various kinds of energy.

For instance, if you burn coal, some of the chemical energy in the coal and the oxygen is released in the form of heat and light. Some of the heat can pass into water, turning it into steam, the hot steam possessing more energy than the original cold water. The energy of the steam can now be converted into kinetic energy (that is, "energy of movement") by allowing it to expand and push a piston which, in turn, causes a generator to revolve. (Not all the energy of the steam goes into moving the piston and the generator. Most of it, in fact, escapes in the form of heat.)

The turning generator converts some of its kinetic energy into electrical energy (again some energy escapes as heat). The electrical energy is conducted along wires to a place where it may be reconverted to kinetic energy when it turns a motor (with more loss as heat). The motor turns this mechanical energy into, for instance, the work of pushing a power saw through the resistance of wood. The

ENERGY CAN BE CONVERTED INTO WORK

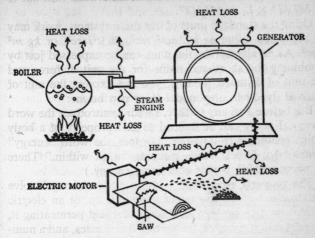

energy involved in the work is partly invested in the conversion of some wood to sawdust (the sawdust containing somewhat more energy than the original wood) but is mostly converted to heat.

If the energy is followed through all its changes, including especially the leakage as heat at each stage, it will be found indeed that the total amount of energy remains the same at every step.

Consequently, physicists took to considering work, together with all forms of energy, as merely different aspects of the same thing. Any units which could be used for work could also be used for any variety of energy, and any units which could be used for one variety of energy could be used for all the other varieties and for work as well.

Consequently, a unit such as $gm\ cm^2/sec^2$ could be used for energy as well as for work. In fact, scientists invented a monosyllable to represent that unit. The monosyllable is *erg* which comes from the Greek word meaning "work" and which is the middle syllable of "energy" so that it well represents both concepts. We can say now:

$$1\ erg = 1\ dyne\text{-}cm = 1gm\ cm^2/sec^2$$

On the other hand, in the *kg-m-sec* system, the unit of work or energy, is *kg m²/sec²* and that is set equal to 1 *joule* (pronounced "jowl"). This is in honor of a British physicist, James Prescott Joule, who, in the 1840's, proved that work could be converted into energy and that a certain amount of work could always be converted into a certain amount of energy. His experiments went a long way toward demonstrating that energy can neither be created nor destroyed, but can only be converted from one form to another, where work is included as one of the forms. This statement is the famous *law of conservation of energy,* one of the most fundamental rules of modern science. So Joule deserves the honor of having a unit named for him.

We can say, then, that:

$$1 \text{ joule} = 1 \text{ newton-}m = 1 \text{ } kg \text{ } m^2/sec^2$$

In the previous chapter, I pointed out that 1 newton was equal to 100,000 dynes. Since, in addition, 1 *m* =100 *cm,* 1 newton-*m* must equal (100,000 dynes) × (100 *cm*) or 10,000,000 dynes-*cm.* Since a newton-*m* is a joule and a dyne-*cm* is an erg:

$$1 \text{ joule} = 10,000,000 \text{ ergs.}$$

Again the convenience of two systems of units involving metric measurements is shown. The erg is a very small unit of energy, which is convenient for use on a small scale. The joule is a much larger unit and is convenient for everyday use.

As for the standard unit of work in the *ft-lb-sec* system, which is *lb ft²/sec²* or the poundal-*ft,* that is infrequently used. Instead, the pound(w)-ft is used. The pound(*w*) is, of course, a unit of force, as I explained in the previous chapter. When multiplied by the foot (a unit of distance) it gives rise to a unit of energy. The only trouble is, the fact that the pound(w) is a unit of weight or force is usually ignored. The pound(w)-*ft* is usually called simply the "foot-pound" and it is natural to assume that the "pound" in the "foot-pound" is the customary "pound" of mass. If it were, the "foot-pound" would be a unit of length multiplied by a unit of mass and that would have the dimensions ML, which are not the dimensions of energy or work.

For the purpose of this book, I will refer to the "foot-pound" as as pound(w)-ft. This may puzzle people who are used to "foot-pounds" but there are times when I would rather be right than customary.

Now a pound(w) is equal to 32.17 poundals, so:

$$1 \text{ pound(w)-}ft = 32.17 \text{ poundal-}ft$$

Since a poundal is equal to 13,825.4 dynes, and a foot is equal to 30.48 cm, it follows that:

$$1 \text{ pound(w)-}ft = 13,580,000 \text{ ergs}$$

And 1 joule is equal to 10,000,00 ergs so:

$$1 \text{ pound(w)-}ft = 1.358 \text{ joules}$$

THE HEATING OF WATER

During the nineteenth century, physicists engaged in the study of heat evolved a new kind of unit. This dealt with the amount of heat it took to raise the temperature of water by a certain amount.

Before I proceed, however, I want to say a few words about temperature. This is a type of measurement which doesn't fit in with the MLT system I am chiefly dealing with in this book. However, it is a type of measurement so familiar to us that it is worth some discussion.

To measure temperature exactly, we need to find some physical change caused by it which we can measure. For instance, when temperature goes up, objects generally expand and when the temperature goes down, they contract. Suppose, then, a bulb were filled with some liquid and this were connected to a thin, evacuated tube. If the bulb were heated, the liquid would expand slightly, and some of it would be forced up the tube. If the tube were thin enough, the liquid would be forced quite a distance up. The height of that thin column of liquid would then change noticeably with even small changes in temperature, rising with heat and falling with cold. This is a "thermometer" (from Greek words meaning "heat measure").

In the seventeenth century, thermometers were invented with water or alcohol as the liquid involved. However, alcohol boiled before temperature got very high and water froze before it got very low. In 1714, a German physicist named Gabriel Daniel Fahrenheit introduced the use of mercury. It stayed liquid at lower temperatures than water did and at higher temperatures than either alcohol or water.

Fahrenheit dipped his mercury thermometer into a mixture of salt and ice and waited for the mercury to sink to some fixed level. He made a scratch on the glass tube at that point and marked it 0. He next dipped the thermometer into boiling water, waited for the mercury to rise to a new level, and marked that 212. The length between he marked off with equally spaced "degrees" (from a Latin word meaning "down steps").

This is the "Fahrenheit scale" of temperature, used today in the English-speaking countries. It is convenient for marking weather changes. In even the coldest winter in

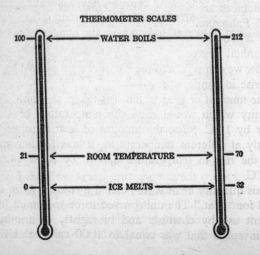

THERMOMETER SCALES

100 ← WATER BOILS → 212

21 ← ROOM TEMPERATURE → 70

0 ← ICE MELTS → 32

the large cities of Europe and America, the temperature rarely drops below 0° and in even the hottest summer it rarely rises above 100°. The freezing point of water on such a scale, as we all know, is 32°.

In 1742, the Swedish astronomer Anders Celsius made use of a different scale. In this, the freezing point of water is 0 and the boiling point 100. This is called the "Centigrade scale" (from Latin words meaning "hundred steps") or the "Celsius scale." The Celsius scale is used in countries other than the English-speaking ones, and is used by scientists everywhere. The reason for this is that the 0 to 100 range just covers the temperatures at which water is liquid. Scientists, especially chemists, work in this range and it is convenient to have it laid out in such a neat decimal fashion.

Temperatures are symbolized as either °F. or °C. depending on which scale is used. Thus the freezing point of water is 32° F. or 0° C., while the boiling point is 212° F. or 100° C.

The distance from the freezing point of water to the boiling point on the Fahrenheit scale is from 32 to 212, or 180 degrees. The same distance on the Celsius scale is from 0 to 100, or 100 degrees. It follows that 180 Fahrenheit degrees are equal to 100 Centigrade degrees, or that 1 4/5 Fahrenheit degrees are equal to one Centigrade degree, while 5/9 of a Centigrade degree is equal to one Fahrenheit degree.

Now we can return to the measurement of heat by means of a rise in temperature——.

The amount of heat which was taken as a unit was that quantity which would raise the temperature of 1 *gm* of water by 1° C. Since the amount of heat required varied slightly at different temperatures, it was further specified that the rise in temperature had to be from 14.5°C. to 15.5°C.

This quantity of heat was called a *calorie,* from a Latin word for "heat." The unit proved to be too small for convenient use by chemists and biologists, so another unit was invented that was equal to 1000 calories. Using the prefix made familiar by the metric system, this larger calorie can be called a *kilocalorie*.

Unfortunately, there is endless confusion here, because the people who use the kilocalorie often do not call it by that name, but use the word "calorie" for it. Sometimes they try to distinguish between the two units by speaking of a "small calorie" and a "large calorie" but more often they say nothing and let confusion reign.

For instance, dietitians and people on diets are always speaking of "calories" and saying that an ounce of butter contains, let us say, 210 "calories" or that a sedentary person uses up 2500 "calories" each day. What they really mean in each case is "kilocalories."

In this book, when I say "calorie" I shall mean the "small calorie" only. The "kilocalorie" is the "large calorie."

Notice that the calorie is based on a gram of water and on 1° C. In England and America, where Fahrenheit degrees are used, engineers often make use of another type of unit. They use as a unit the amount of heat required to raise the temperature of 1 *lb* of water by 1° F. (from 59½° F. to 60½° F., to be exact). This unit is called the *British Thermal Unit* ("thermal" coming from a Greek word for "heat") and this is commonly abbreviated as *BTU*.

Now 1 *lb* = 453.592 *gm* and 1° F. = 0.545° C. This means that in the case of the BTU you are heating 453.592 times as much water as in the case of the calorie through a rise of 0.545 times the temperature. Therefore, 1 BTU = 453.592 × 0.545 or:

$$1 \text{ BTU} = 252.0 \quad \text{calories}$$
$$1 \text{ BTU} = \quad 0.252 \text{ kilocalorie}$$

To put it another way:

$$1 \text{ kilocalorie} = 3.97 \text{ BTU}$$

Once it was understood that heat was a form of energy and could be expressed in the usual units used for other forms of energy, it was realized that such units as calories, kilocalories, and BTU's should be convertible into ergs, joules, pounds(w)-*ft,* and so on.

By actual measurement, Joule found that 41,850,000 ergs could be converted into 1 calorie of heat. From this, using the various conversion factors given in this book, it follows that:

$$1 \text{ calorie} = 41,850,000 \text{ ergs} = 4.185 \text{ joules}$$
$$1 \text{ kilocalorie} = 41,850,000,000 \text{ ergs} = 4185 \text{ joules}$$
$$1 \text{ BTU} = 10,550,000,000 \text{ ergs} = 1055 \text{ joules}$$

Since 1 pound(w)-*ft* is equal to 1.358 joules, we can also say that:

$$1 \text{ calorie} = 3.082 \text{ pounds(w)-}ft$$
$$1 \text{ kilocalorie} = 3082 \text{ pounds(w)-}ft$$
$$1 \text{ BTU} = 778 \text{ pounds(w)-}ft$$

Now this explains one reason why it is so difficult to reduce by exercise alone. To expend 1 pound(w)-*ft* of energy, you must raise a weight of one pound the distance of one foot against gravity. To expend 1 kilocalorie of energy, you must then do this 3082 times since 1 kilocalorie equals 3082 pounds(w)-*ft*.

Or, if you yourself weigh 154 pounds(w), you must jump 1 *ft* upward 20 times, since 154 pounds(w) × 1*ft* × 20 = 3080 pounds(w)-*ft.* Another way of saying it is that if you weigh 154 pounds(w), you must run up two flights of stairs, each of which is 10 feet high all told, in order to use up the equivalent of 1 kilocalorie of energy.

Since a pat of butter contains about 50 kilocalories of energy, you must go up 100 flights of stairs to use up the energy content you have gained by eating the pat. It would seem easier not to eat the pat in the first place, wouldn't it? (I am not trying to preach. I know this kind of advice falls on deaf ears. I am overweight myself.)

THE STRENGTH OF HORSES

Energy (or work) can be delivered at varying rates. Imagine yourself running up a flight of stairs. If you weigh

150 pounds and the flight is 10 feet high in the vertical direction, then you have used up 1500 pounds(w)-*ft* in doing so.

It doesn't matter whether you take a minute to do it or a day. The same amount of energy is used up in the process since that only depends on the weight you lift (*i.e.*, the force you exert) and the distance through which the weight is lifted (or the forces exerted).

(Of course, you will be using up energy in other respects, too. Energy is consumed in breathing, in keeping your heart beating and kidneys working and so on. However, I am only talking about the energy used in actually lifting your body up the stairs.)

Nevertheless, although the energy expended is the same regardless of the time you take, there is a difference of some sort. If you walk up slowly and take several minutes, you reach the top of the flight in perfect comfort. If you run up at top speed and take only a few seconds, you are out of breath and puff and become hot.

The rate at which energy is expended is referred to as *power*. You may be expending the same energy and doing the same work when you run up the stairs, but you are exerting far more power then than if you walk up. Similarly, a machine that can lift a weight a given distance (or do any other form of work) quickly has more power than one that can only do this slowly.

Power, then, may be considered as the work performed per unit time. The dimensions of work are ML^2/T^2. Work per time would therefore be $(ML^2/T^2)/T$, or ML^2/T^3.

In the three systems I have been discussing, the unit of power may be expressed as $gm\ cm^2/sec^3$, $lb\ ft^2/sec^3$, and $kg\ m^2/sec^3$. An equivalent way of expressing these units is to make use of the special names already developed for the corresponding units of work. For instance, the unit of energy in the *gm-cm-sec* system is the erg. In that system, then, the unit of power would be erg/*sec*. Analogously, the unit of power in the other two systems would be poundal-*ft*/*sec* and joule/*sec*.

Since, in forming units of power in the three systems, we have only added a "per second" to each of the corresponding units for energy or work, the conversion factors remain the same. In other words, since 1 joule = 10,000,-000 ergs, then 1 joule/*sec* = 10,000,000 erg/*sec*.

The most common everyday unit of power, at least in the English-speaking countries, is none of these, however, but is one which was invented by James Watt, who developed the first practical steam engine.

Watt's steam engine was first used for pumping water out of mines. In the days before the steam engine, this task had been performed by horses. Watt, then, was interested in comparing the power of his steam engine to that of a horse. (Just lifting the water out of the mine wasn't enough; it had to be removed fast enough to keep up with the rate of seepage. Power, not just work, was what counted.)

Watt set strong draft-horses to work lifting weights. From the results, he calculated that a good strong horse could do work at the rate of 550 pound(w)-*ft*/*sec*. Ever since, this rate of doing work has been termed a *horsepower* (even though very few horses can deliver that power). Watt rated his steam engines in horsepower and we still rate the engines of automobiles and airplanes in horsepower to this day.

Now what is a horsepower in standard units of the three systems I have been discussing? Earlier in the chapter, I said that a pound(w)-*ft* = 32.17 poundal-*ft*. Consequently 550 pound(w)-*ft* is equal to (550 × 32.17 poundal-*ft*) / *sec*, so that:

$$1 \text{ horsepower} = 17,690 \text{ poundal-}ft/sec$$

Since 1 pound(w)-*ft* = 13,580,00 ergs = 1.358 joules, a horsepower (which is equal to 550 pound(w)-*ft*/*sec*) must be equal to (550 × 1.358 joule)/*sec*. Or:

$$1 \text{ horsepower} = 7,460,000,000 \text{ erg}/sec$$
$$1 \text{ horsepower} = 746 \text{ joule}/sec$$

A unit of power similar to the horsepower is also used in countries that use the metric system. The French call is *cheval-vapeur* ("horse-steam") but in English it is usually called *metric horsepower*. The metric horsepower can be expressed in much the same way ordinary horsepower is, except that instead of feet and pounds(w), meters and kilograms(w) are used.

A metric horsepower is set equal to 4500 kilogram(w)-*m* per minute and this comes out to 75 kilogram(w)-*m/sec*.

Since 1 *m* = 3.28 *ft* and 1 kilogram(w) = 2.205 pounds (w), 1 metric horsepower equals (75 × 3.28 *ft* × 2.205 pounds(w))/*sec*. This is (75 × 3.28 × 2.205) pound (w)-*ft/sec*, so that:

$$1 \text{ metric horsepower} = 542.4 \text{ pound(w)-}ft/sec$$

But an ordinary horsepower is equal to 550 pound(w)-*ft/sec*, so it is slightly greater than a metric horsepower. In fact, 1 horsepower equals 550/542.4 metric horsepower, or:

$$1 \text{ horsepower} = 1.014 \text{ metric horsepower}$$

Since 1 horsepower is equal to 746 joule/*sec*, 1 metric horsepower must be equal to 746/1.014 joule/*sec*, or:

$$1 \text{ metric horsepower} = 735 \ 1/2 \text{ joule/}sec$$

LIGHT BULBS AND HUMAN BEINGS

The joule/*sec* has received a special name, one which rightly honors the first man to go about the systematic measurement of power. The joule/*sec* is called the *watt* (and, fortunately, James Watt was thoughtful enough to have a one-syllable name). Thus:

$$1 \text{ watt} = 1 \text{ joule/}sec = 1 \text{ kg } m^2/sec^3$$

Wherever I have used joule/*sec* in my conversions in the previous section, I can substitute watts. Thus:

$$1 \text{ watt} = 10,000,000 \text{ erg/}sec$$
$$1 \text{ horsepower} = 746 \text{ watts}$$

Watts are most familiar to us in connection with ~~electrical~~ equipment. A hundred-watt light bulb consumes electrical energy and delivers light energy and heat energy at the rate of 100 joules/*sec*.

Watts are a metric unit involving kilograms and meters (one of the few metric units in common use in the English-speaking countries, though few of the population are aware of this). Consequently, the watt will naturally take the usual prefixes used in the metric system. There are deci-watts, centiwatts, and so on. The most familiar of this type of unit is the *kilowatt,* and, of course:

$$1 \quad \text{kilowatt} = 1000 \text{ watts}$$

Since a horsepower is equal to 746 watts, a kilowatt is equal to 1000/746 horsepower. In other words:

$$1 \quad \text{kilowatt} = 1.34 \text{ horsepower}$$

We can get back from power to energy, if we multiply the power unit by time. Thus 1 joule/*sec* × 1 *sec* = 1 joule-*sec/sec* or, canceling the *sec* above and below the fraction line, 1 joule. Since 1 joule/*sec* = 1 watt, we may as well say:

$$1 \text{ watt-}sec = 1 \text{ joule.}$$

A more common unit of energy of this sort is the *kilowatt-hour.* Since a kilowatt is equal to 1000 watts and an hour is equal to 3600 *sec,* a kilowatt-hour equals 1000 × 3600 or 3,600,000 watt-*sec*. We can say then:

$$1 \quad \text{kilowatt-hour} = 3,600,000 \text{ joules}$$

The kilowatt-hour is therefore the largest unit of energy I have yet discussed.

Since, as I said earlier in the chapter, 1 kilocalorie = 4185 joules, 1 kilowatt-hour equals 3,600,000/4185 kilocalories, or:

$$1 \quad \text{kilowatt-hour} = 860 \text{ kilocalories}$$

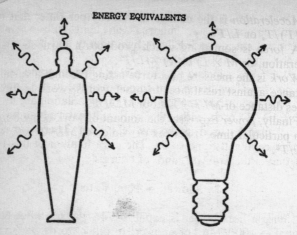

Now the average human being can get along comfortably on 2500 kilocalories per day. This is the equivalent of 2500/860 or just about 3 kilowatt-hours per day. Having consumed that much energy, he gives it off again, mostly as heat.

Consider next that a 125-watt light bulb delivers in 24 hours 125 × 24, or 3000 watt-hours. This is equal to 3 kilowatt-hours.

Thus, each human being delivers as much heat to his surroundings, on the average, as would a 125-watt light bulb. If you have ever been in a crowded place on a warm day, you will appreciate what this means.

TO SUMMARIZE

Suppose I stop here for a moment, before going on with the last chapter of the book, just to take a backward glance over the path we have traveled.

We began with *length* (*L*), *mass* (*M*), and *time* (*T*). *Distance* is measured in length, so its dimensions are *L*.

Velocity is the amount of distance (in a particular direction) covered in a certain amount of time. It is in other words, distance per time, or *L/T*.

Acceleration is the change in velocity per time; that is, $(L/T)/T$, or L/T^2.

A *force* is something which produces a particular acceleration, or $M \times L/T^2$, or ML/T^2.

Work is the measure of a force acting through a certain distance against resistance. In other words, work is force times distance or $ML/T^2 \times L$, or ML^2/T^2.

Finally, *power* expresses the amount of work being done in a particular time. It is work per time or $(ML^2/T^2)/T$, or ML/T^3.

. . .

10 10 10 10 10 10 10 10 10 10

Poises and Quanta

CONSTANTS

I have by no means exhausted the types of units used
by scientists. I have already mentioned temperature, for
instance, as involving units I have no room to discuss in
detail. Units involved in such properties as light intensity
or sound intensity exist, too, as well as a whole family of
units involved in electrical and magnetic phenomena. For
none of these is there room.

All can be fitted logically into the systems so far de-
scribed. They do not represent new principles, only exten-
sions of old ones.

Before leaving the subject and ending the book, however, I would like to spend some time considering examples
of how units play a part in some of the fundamental relationships discovered by scientists.

Scientists like to describe the universe by means of
mathematical relationships that are as simple as possible.
They are particularly pleased when they can find a series
of measurements that can be so arranged as to give an
answer that does not change when the values of the individual measurements are changed.

The measurements that change are *variables,* while the
answer that remains the same is a *constant.*

A simple example of what I mean arises in connection
with density, which I have already discussed in Chapter 7.

Consider water. You can have any mass of water—1 gm,
10 gm, 1000 gm, 1,000,000,000 gm. The mass of water
is a variable and each particular sample of water must be
weighed separately if its mass is to be known.

Similarly, you can have any volume of water—1 cm^3,
10 cm^3, 1000 cm^3, 1,000,000,000 cm^3. This is another

variable and its value, too, must be determined separately for each sample of water.

However, suppose we divide the mass of a sample of water by its volume to get the density. It turns out that 1 *gm* of water has a volume of 1 cm^3; 10 *gm* has a volume of 10 cm^3; 1000 *gm* has one of 1000 cm^3; 1,000,000,000 *gm* one of 1,000,000,000 cm^3, and so on. In each case, mass divided by volume gives an answer of 1 gm/cm^3.

The density is therefore a constant (at least for a given substance under given conditions). If someone hands you a container of water, you cannot know either its mass or volume until it is measured, but you do know its density.

Let's take a more complicated case. You know from experience that some liquids pour more easily than others. Tip a glass of water and it will pour out quickly. Tip a glass of castor oil and it will pour out slowly.

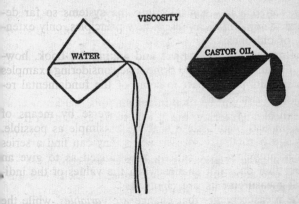

VISCOSITY

WATER

CASTOR OIL

In the pouring out of any liquid, some molecules of the liquid must slide over other molecules under the pull of gravity. The more easily the sliding takes place, the more quickly does the liquid spill. Water molecules slide over each other much more easily than the molecules of castor oil and therefore pour more quickly.

But scientists aren't satisfied with just saying "more easily." They want to find some way of measuring exactly the ease or difficulty with which molecules slide past one another in different liquids. They set up experiments that will tell them upon what this ease or difficulty depends.

Suppose, for instance, you imagine two layers of liquid, each in the form of a square of a particular area. These layers are parallel to each other and are a certain distance apart. Now suppose that some force is applied to one of the layers, causing it to slip and slide over the other. As a result it will move at some certain velocity.

It turned out, upon experiment, that if the force were multiplied by the distance between the layers and this were divided by the velocity times the area of the layers, the same answer always resulted for a particular liquid at a particular temperature. In other words:

$$\frac{\text{force} \times \text{distance}}{\text{velocity} \times \text{area}} = \text{a constant}$$

This constant is called *viscosity,* and its value describes the ease or difficulty with which molecules of a liquid slide over other molecules of the same liquid. The constant for castor oil is higher than for water; therefore castor oil is said to have a higher viscosity than water, or to be more viscous.

The viscosity can be used in calculations that are useful in chemical engineering, but if it is to be used, its correct dimensions must be used. What, then, are the dimensions of viscosity?

By using the relationship that gives the constant (see above), and substituting the dimensions of each measurement, you will end with the dimensions of viscosity.

The dimensions of force are ML/T^2, those of distance are L, of velocity L/T, and of area L^2. If we multiply the dimensions of force by those of distance and divide that by the dimensions of velocity times those of area, we will have the dimensions of the constant we are calling viscosity.

$$\frac{ML/T^2 \times L}{L/T \times L^2} = M/LT$$

(I want to remind you that these letters are symbols and

can be treated like any other algebraic symbols. You may wonder, now and then, if this is really so. Well, let's take a simple example. If you multiply 4 feet by 6 feet, you have 24 square feet, as you will admit. You can symbolize this by saying:

$$24 \ ft^2 = 4 \ ft \times 6 \ ft$$

But you can convert any multiplication to a division by shifting one of the terms to the other side of the equation. That gives you a second statement which is equivalent to the one above:

$$24 \ ft^2/4 \ ft = 6 \ ft$$

To get the 6 in the answer, you need only divide 24 by 4 and see for yourself that that part of the equation remains true. As for the units, you can only conclude that $ft^2/ft = ft$, just as $x^2/x = x$. If you tackle other relationships involving units, you will find that in every case the symbols representing the units will behave just like other algebraic symbols.)

The dimensions of viscosity (obtained by elementary algebra) are M/LT and, in the three systems of units I have been discussing, the units of viscosity are $gm/cm \ sec$, $kg/m \ sec$, and $lb/ft \ sec$.

The first to study viscosity methodically was the French scientist Jean Louis Marie Poiseuille. His name has been given to the unit of viscosity in the gm-cm-sec system, but (fortunately for those of us not born to the French language) only the first syllable of his name was used, i.e., poise. Consequently:

$$1 \ gm/cm \ sec = 1 \ poise$$

Actually, the poise is somewhat too large to be a convenient unit and a hundredth of a poise, or a *centipoise*, is more commonly used. For instance, the viscosity of water at room temperature is just about one centipoise. In comparison, castor oil at room temperature has a viscosity of about 1000 centipoises (which is equivalent to 10 poises).

Air, at room temperature, on the other hand, has a viscosity of only about 185 *micropoises*. A micropoise is a millionth of a poise, or a ten-thousandth of a centipoise, so that is equivalent to 0.0185 centipoises.

NEWTON AND CAVENDISH

For a more fundamental example, let's go back again to 1683, when Isaac Newton published the book containing his Laws of Motion, which I mentioned in Chapter 8. In this book, *Principia Mathematica,* he also proclaimed his Law of Universal Gravitation.

To see how this law works, let's consider two bodies. They can be any two bodies; two steel balls an inch apart, the earth and the moon, the sun and a far-distant star, any two bodies at all. According to Newton's suggestion, there is an attractive force between these two bodies which depends upon the mass of each body and upon the square of the distance between them. (The force goes up as the masses increase and goes down as the distance increases.)

Furthermore, Newton's theory worked out in such a way that if the gravitational force between two bodies were multiplied by the square of the distance between them and this were divided by the mass of the first body times the mass of the second, the result would be a constant (called the *gravitational constant*). To summarize this:

$$\frac{\text{gravitational force} \times \text{distance}^2}{\text{mass-one} \times \text{mass-two}} = \text{constant}$$

Newton showed that the gravitational constant had the same value for the earth and the moon as for the earth and an apple falling from a tree. It was his guess (he had no way of proving it) that the gravitational constant had the same value everywhere in the universe.

In the 1700's, a succession of astronomers showed that the gravitational constant was the same throughout the solar system because only so could the motion of the planets about the sun be explained exactly. Finally, in the 1800's, astronomers checked the motions of double stars about each other and found that the gravitational constant appeared to be the same throughout the galaxy.

Now what are the dimensions of this gravitational constant that seems to be built into the very fabric of matter? We can determine that from the equation that establishes the constant, just substituting the dimensions of each variable mentioned.

For instance, the dimensions of gravitational force, as of any force, are ML/T^2. The dimension of distance is L, so the dimension of the square of a distance is L^2. The dimension of mass is M, so the dimensions of the mass of one body times the mass of another are $M \times M$, or M^2. Substituting these dimensions into the equation given earlier in this section then, we have:

$$\frac{ML/T^2 \times L^2}{M^2} = \frac{L^3}{MT^2}$$

The unit of the gravitational constant can be set up according to either side of this equation. The right-hand side, L^3/MT^2, is simpler, and in the *gm-cm-sec* system the units of the gravitational constant would be $cm^3/gm\ sec^2$. More often, though, it is the left-hand side that is used. Since ML/T^2 is the unit of force, this comes out to force-L^2/M, and in the *gm-cm-sec* system, this would be dyne-cm^2/gm^2.

Now the exact value of the gravitational constant was never known to Newton. The first man to determine it was the English scientist Henry Cavendish, who in 1798 measured the attraction between two metal balls and calculated the gravitational constant from that. The value which is now considered most accurate on the basis of modern measurements is 0.0000000667 dynes -cm^2/gm^2.

This means that if two bodies, each 1 gram in mass, were placed 1 centimeter apart (as measured from center to center) they would attract each other with a gravitational force of 0.0000000667 dynes. Since a dyne is equal to 1.02 milligrams (w) or 0.00102 grams(w), it means that if those two bodies were all that existed in the universe, each one would weigh 0.000000000068 grams under the gravitational attraction of each other.

But each of those bodies weighs 1 gram under the gravitational attraction of the earth, even though the center of the earth is fully 4000 miles from those bodies so that its gravitational force is correspondingly weakened. To have that much more of an attraction at that much greater distance, the earth must have a tremendously greater mass. In fact, the mass of the earth can be calculated from this difference in gravitational force and turns out to be about 6,000,000,000,000,000,000,000,000,000 grams.

If you look back on the reasoning in the last few paragraphs, you will see that the earth cannot have its mass measured until the value of the gravitational constant is determined. Thus, when Cavendish became the first to determine the value of this constant, he also became the first ever to "weigh the earth."

PLANCK

In 1900, the German physicist Max Planck advanced his Quantum Theory, which revolutionized science. The Quantum Theory suggests that energy can only exist in little packets or *quanta,* and in whole numbers of those. In other words, you might get 1 quantum of energy, or 2 quanta, or 3 quanta, but you could never get 1½ quanta or 2½ quanta. All theories involving energy had to be revised in light of this new concept since previously scientists had believed that energy could be delivered in any quantities at all.

(Of course, the quantum is such a super-tiny bit of energy that in ordinary life we never notice the fact that there are certain amounts of energy we can't get. The least bit of energy we will notice ordinarily involves many trillions of quanta. Who would notice that we might have, say 1,000,000,000,000 quanta delivered or 1,000,000,-000,001 quanta, but never 1,000,000,000,000 1/2 quanta?)

Planck's theory concerned itself also with just how large the quantum was. (In fact, the word *quantum* is Latin for "how much?".) Planck decided that the size must vary with the type of energy involved. For instance, the quantum of red light is only half the size of the quantum of violet light.

Now red light and violet light are both forms of radiant energy which behaves as though it consists of tiny waves in space. The waves can be of various lengths. The smaller the *wave lengths,* the more waves can be formed in one second as light speeds along. The number of waves formed in one second is called the *frequency*.

The wave length of violet light is about half that of red light. Violet light can therefore form twice as many of those "half-size" waves in one second as red light will of the "full-size" ones. Violet light thus has twice the frequency that red light has.

Planck showed that the larger the frequency, the larger the quantum of the light wave possessing that frequency, and in exact proportion. If you halved the frequency, you halved the size of the quantum; if you doubled one, you doubled the other and so on.

This means that the size of the quantum divided by the frequency of the energy involved is a constant—one which is called *Planck's constant*.

Now the dimensions of the quantum are those of energy, since the quantum is merely a quantity of energy, and is therefore ML^2/T^2. The dimensions of frequency, which is expressed as "so many wave lengths per second," are similar to the case I presented in Chapter 6, of the "so many revolutions per second." This is also a case of reciprocal seconds and the dimensions of frequency are therefore $1/T$.

To get Planck's constant, we must divide the size of the quantum by the frequency of the energy. Therefore, to get ML^2/T^2 by $1/T$, and this comes to ML^2/T.
the dimensions of Planck's constant, we must divide
Measurements that have this dimension are said to be expressed in units of *action*. Planck's constant (the "quantum of action") would have units, in the *gm-cm-sec* system of *gm cm²/sec*.

Now an erg is equal to $gm\ cm^2/sec^2$. If this is multiplied by time, you have $gm\ cm^2/sec^2 \times sec,$ which comes out to *gm-cm-sec*. (Thus energy × time = action.) Consequently, on the *gm-cm-sec* system, the units of Planck's constant can be expressed as erg-*sec*.

Now the frequency of violet light turns out to be about 750,000,000,000,000/*sec*. This is an extremely large number, but then Planck's constant is an extremely small one. Planck's constant, in fact, is equal to 0.00000000000000-0000000000006624 erg-*sec*. Multiply this by the frequency of violet light and we find that 750,000,000,000-000/*sec* × 0.00000000000000000000000006624 erg-*sec* is equal to just about 0.000000000005 ergs. That is the amount of energy contained in one quantum of violet light. It follows from this that one erg of violet light contains 200,000,000,000 quanta.

Since the frequency of red light is half that of violet light, the energy contained in a quantum of red light is only half that contained in a quantum of violet light. Therefore, one erg of red light contains, 400,000,000,000 quanta.

What is important is not so much the number of quanta that impinges upon matter every second as the size of the individual quanta. That is why violet light can affect an ordinary photographic plate while red light cannot, so that it is possible to work in darkrooms that are lit by red light without fogging film.

As light of frequency higher than violet light is considered, the individual quanta get larger too. Ultraviolet is made up of quanta larger than violet light. The quanta of X rays are larger still and the quanta of gamma rays still larger. The quanta of some gamma rays may be a billion times as large as the quanta of violet light.

It is these larger quanta that make it possible for ultraviolet to redden the skin and allow X rays and gamma rays to penetrate matter and be deadly to life. Exposure to gamma rays as compared with exposure to red light is like being bombarded with baseballs instead of with feathers.

EINSTEIN

In 1905, the German-born physicist Albert Einstein advanced his Theory of Relativity which showed, among other things, that mass could be converted into energy and vice versa. Furthermore, a quantity of mass could only be converted to a certain quantity of energy. Double the quantity of mass and you get just double the amount of energy.

This is equivalent to saying that the amount of energy you get divided by the amount of mass you start with always gives the same result; that is, a constant.

As usual, let's ask what the dimensions of this constant are. We are dividing energy by mass to get the constant, so we must divide the dimensions of energy by the dimensions of mass to get the dimensions of the constant. The dimensions of energy are ML^2/T^2 and the dimensions of mass are M. If we divide ML^2/T^2 by M, we get L^2/T^2 and those must be the dimensions of *Einstein's constant*.

We know that the dimensions of velocity are L/T (as I explained in Chapter 7). Since L^2/T^2 is the square of L/T, we can say that the dimensions of Einstein's constant are equal to those of the square of a velocity.

Einstein showed just this and showed, moreover, that the particular velocity that had to be squared was the velocity of light. Consequently, energy divided by mass is equal to the square of the velocity of light. If you let energy be symbolized as e, mass as m, and the velocity of light as

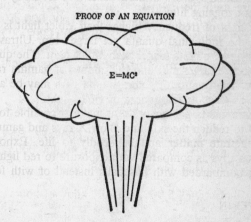

PROOF OF AN EQUATION

$E = MC^2$

c, you can represent the above statement as $e/m = c^2$. And if you clear fractions according to the usual rule in algebra, you end with Einstein's equation, now very famous: $e = mc^2$. (Notice that m can stand either for "mass" or for "meter." This sort of thing is common in science and often creates confusion. I have tried to avoid such confusion in this book, but here at the very end, I have been trapped.)

If we use the *gm-cm-sec* system, the velocity of light would have to be expressed in *cm/sec,* and this comes out to just about 30,000,000,000 *cm/sec* (see page 97). The square of that value is 900,000,000,000,000,000,000 *cm²/sec²* so that Einstein's constant is huge indeed.

If we multiply Einstein's constant by 1 gram, the result is 900,000,000,000,000,000,000 *gm cm²/sec².* Since the *gm cm²/sec²* is equal to the erg, we can say that, by Einstein's equation:

$$1 \ gm = 900{,}000{,}000{,}000{,}000{,}000{,}000 \ \text{ergs}$$

To receive nine hundred billion billion ergs of energy from one small gram of matter is something that is hard to believe, but the hydrogen bomb, which results from the conversion of some mass into energy, is ample and horrifying proof that Eeinstein's theory is correct.

If we used the *kg-m-sec* system, we would express the speed of light in *m/sec;* that is, as 300,000,000 *m/sec.* The square of that velocity is 90,000,000,000,000,000 *m²/sec².* Multiply that by 1 *kg* and the result is 90,000,000,000,-000,000 *kg m²/sec².* This last unit is equivalent to the joule, so:

$$1 \ kg = 90{,}000{,}000{,}000{,}000{,}000{,} \ \text{joules}$$

Since one kilowatt-hour equals 3,600,000 joules, 1 kilogram of mass is the equivalent of 90,000,000,000,000,-000/3,600,000 kilowatt-hours. Therefore:

$$1 \ kg = 25{,}000{,}000{,}000 \ \text{kilowatt-hours}$$

and, of course,

$$1 \ gm = 25{,}000{,}000 \ \text{kilowatt-hours.}$$

That means that if 1 gram of mass were completely con-

erted into energy, there would be enough energy produced
o keep a 1000-watt light bulb burning brightly for 25,000,-
000 hours, or for about 2850 years.

The theories of Newton, Planck, and Einstein are fundamental to theoretical physics. Yet, you see even in the
highest rarefactions of thought, it is as important—and as
helpful—to keep the units straight as it was the first time
some early farmer tried to pace off the boundaries of his
farm.

INDEX